UNIVERSITY OF MINNESOTA
STUDIES OF GENERAL EDUCATION

Malcolm S. MacLean, editor

THEY WENT TO COLLEGE: A STUDY OF
951 FORMER UNIVERSITY STUDENTS

by C. Robert Pace

THESE WE TEACH: A STUDY OF
GENERAL COLLEGE STUDENTS

by Cornelia T. Williams

BUILDING A CURRICULUM FOR GENERAL
EDUCATION: A DESCRIPTION OF THE
GENERAL COLLEGE PROGRAM

by Ivol Spafford and Others

OUTCOMES OF GENERAL EDUCATION: AN APPRAISAL
OF THE GENERAL COLLEGE PROGRAM

by Ruth E. Eckert

Outcomes of General Education

An Appraisal of the General College Program

by

RUTH E. ECKERT

ASSOCIATE PROFESSOR OF EDUCATION AND ASSOCIATE DIRECTOR
OF THE COMMITTEE ON EDUCATIONAL RESEARCH AND OF THE
BUREAU OF EDUCATIONAL RESEARCH, UNIVERSITY OF MINNESOTA

THE UNIVERSITY OF MINNESOTA PRESS

Minneapolis

Acknowledgments

This evaluation study has been a cooperative project from start to finish. Members of the General College administration, faculty, and student body have contributed their time, as have a host of people outside the college. Hence it is almost impossible for the writer to acknowledge all the counsel and assistance she has received.

Evaluation of the General College program was first conceived by Malcolm S. MacLean, then director of the college and now president of Hampton Institute, and by Ivol Spafford, at that time director of curriculum revision in the General College. The necessary funds were supplied by the General Education Board of the Rockefeller Foundation, which has also supported the General College curriculum and personnel studies. In assisting the writer to plan and conduct this appraisal Dean MacLean and Miss Spafford both gave generously of their time throughout the entire two-year period of the study. Similar aid was received from members of an advisory committee appointed by Guy Stanton Ford, then acting president of the university, to guide its development. The writer is especially indebted to the members of this committee — Dean MacLean, Wilford S. Miller, Edgar B. Wesley, Donald G. Paterson, and T. Raymond McConnell, chairman — for counsel on many difficult problems.

Although the investigation was not begun until September 1938, the staff of the General College had already laid considerable groundwork for such a study, as is explained in Chapter 2. Every member of that staff contributed substantially to the project through such activities as outlining objectives, constructing and criticizing evaluation instruments, and suggesting many sources of evidence concerning the strengths and weaknesses of this experimental curriculum. Indeed without all the help af-

v

21104

forded by General College instructors and counselors the study could not have been made. Students, too, willingly participated in tests and interviews and through their Student Council conducted a careful study of young people's opinions of the General College program.

In gathering, analyzing, and interpreting the data upon which the present study rests, the writer was greatly aided by Blanche G. Anderson, statistical clerk, who served on half time for two years; Bessie S. Smith, graduate student in psychometrics, who likewise gave half her time to this study during 1938–39; and C. Robert Pace, who served as research associate on a half-time basis during 1939–40. Clinical assistance was furnished by WPA personnel and by university NYA students. C. Harold Stone and Nicholas A. Fattu, who were conducting studies of the General College vocational and individual orientation courses, contributed much to the appraisal of outcomes in these areas.

After the first draft of the manuscript had been prepared, the writer obtained many helpful suggestions from Dean MacLean, Miss Spafford, and Horace T. Morse, the present associate director of the General College. Mr. Pace, now evaluation consultant for the Commission on Teacher Education, also read it critically, and because of his close association with the project during its second year made suggestions that have helped immeasurably in revising the manuscript.

The present study is only a first exploratory effort to find out what has been achieved by one general education program designed especially for young people of just average scholastic ability. As is pointed out many times in the succeeding pages, it is in no sense an adequate or comprehensive evaluation; instruments were lacking to measure many important outcomes, and the time and the resources for making such a study were extremely limited. The writer's chief hope is that, despite its many limitations, this book may help in pointing the way to appraisal studies that will actually demonstrate what our colleges are now doing for young people and what they have yet failed to do.

R. E. E.

Editor's Foreword

From the beginning of the General College in the fall of 1932, its administration and its staff insisted on evaluation; we wanted to know what we were getting for what we were doing. We were keenly aware of what we had set out to do, for two serious problems had led President Coffman to authorize the establishment of the college as a new and independent unit of the University of Minnesota:

First, the long-time and powerful tendency in higher education for the curriculum to grow like a cancer, by a process of cell division with no powers of elimination. At Minnesota the growth was so great that slightly more than 600 courses were open to freshmen and sophomores. This was obviously an ill that no amount of personnel and guidance work could cure, since the ability to know 600 courses well, to diagnose a student's capacities, needs, and interests, and to join these two in a sensible program lies beyond the powers of either high school or college counselors. In the General College, therefore, we were to see what we could do experimentally to synthesize the many fragments of learning into an effective general education for the freshman and sophomore years.

Second, an almost universal tendency on the part of any teaching staff to assume that each year's crop of students is lower in intelligence, interest, and the desire to achieve than the previous year's crop. Related to this is the notion that a student who does not succeed in one subject will probably be poor in all fields. In the General College, therefore, we had to find out whether the human beings considered slag and scrap by other teachers and administrators were susceptible to salvage. When a student is declared a misfit, we asked, is *he* the misfit or are the courses which he has chosen, or into which he has been put, unfit for him? Or are there other causes, such as poverty, poor family conditions, neurotic worry, and many more, that now or forever make him unable to take any of the university's offerings with profit?

It was our problem, then, to know our students as fully as they could be known with the personnel techniques available to us. It was our problem, knowing our students, to devise a comparatively simplified, sturdy, valuable curriculum in general education. To solve these problems we must build a thoroughly adequate personnel and guidance service; fashion a curriculum; train and supervise instructors; develop the best possible examinations; and, while carrying on all these things, try to test the value of each process to the students, the college, the university, and the state.

During the early years of the college our evaluation consisted of much preliminary observation, self-searching, checking against the work of other experimental colleges such as Wisconsin, Chicago, Stephens, Reed, Sarah Lawrence, Pasadena Junior College, and others. The university's Committee on Educational Research supplied us with a continuous flow of investigations and reports on our progress, including two volumes of evaluation. Then we began to publish the results of our own studies. The other three books in the current series—Dr. Pace's *They Went to College*, Dr. Williams' *These We Teach*, and Dr. Spafford's *Building a Curriculum*—reveal various insights into what we did, and why, and what we got for it.

The present volume is a notable addition to what has been done, and what is to be done, in determining the value of our attempts to be intelligent in furthering and guiding a small part of the revolution that is taking place in American higher education. In the pages that follow, Dr. Eckert unfolds the arduous, difficult, and limited task of evaluating a very young college. It was a college that could not and would not hold still while tape measure and weighing machine were applied. Unfortunately there are as yet no educational stroboscopes, no colorimeters or other instruments giving sure results. But within the limitations of great activity and change on the part of the college and its milieu, as well as the limitations of crude or new or undeveloped instruments, Dr. Eckert has come out with an evaluation picture of the General College that has some solidity and form. More than that — and this is perhaps the best contribution of any attempt at evaluation of great complexity — it indicates with real specificity the directions in which, and some of the means by which, further evaluation can be made.

MALCOLM S. MACLEAN
President, Hampton Institute
Hampton, Virginia

Table of Contents

List of Figures

Outcomes of General Education

CHAPTER I

The General College at the University of Minnesota

Almost a million young people graduate from the high schools of America each year; another million and a half withdraw before completing the secondary school program. Of all these young people — those who receive diplomas and those who do not — less than a fifth continue their education on a full-time basis in some other institution. For the vast majority of them secondary education has been terminal education. Furthermore since only one out of every two students who go from high school into college receive diplomas or degrees, it is evident that whatever final preparation is to be given for out-of-school living must be provided in the upper years of the secondary school or the early years of the college. This book is essentially an appraisal of one such program, especially designed to give young people the help they need in meeting present and future problems.

THE SECONDARY SCHOOL'S RESPONSIBILITY FOR GENERAL EDUCATION

Yet despite the fact that the twentieth century has seen a tremendous change in both the size and the nature of the American high school student body, from a small, highly selected group seeking primarily preparation for college to a vastly larger group seeking final vocational and cultural training, few fundamental alterations have been made in high school curriculums. The hazards and perplexities involved in meeting personal problems, in finding jobs, in establishing one's self and one's family, and in participating intelligently in democratic processes — all these have commonly been ignored. Such deviations from the college pre-

NOTE. Assistance in the preparation of these materials was furnished by the personnel of Work Projects Administration Official Project No. 165-1-71-124, Subproject No. 334.

paratory program as are offered by commercial or industrial subjects appear too often as mere devices to lend respectability to lowered academic standards, or as reluctant token courses rather than thoughtful efforts to provide for the diverse talents and needs of young people. For the responsibilities as parents, workers, and citizens that must within a few years confront practically all these young people — those who go on to college and those who do not — the traditional curriculum of the secondary school has provided little systematic preparation. Recent studies of youth and its problems have consistently brought to light some highly disquieting conditions, emphasizing again and again the lost opportunities of the secondary school.[1] Yet these findings do not constitute an indictment of the institution, for too often the school simply reflects the social demands made upon it.

Obviously, then, a new educational program must be evolved for the vast majority of young people who do not continue beyond the secondary school, a program realistically adapted to both the potentialities of these adolescents and the needs of our rapidly changing social order — one planned in terms of the life goals of the students instead of the conventional academic patterns. Fortunately, hopeful signs of such reorganization within the secondary school have appeared in recent years, as individual schools develop broader conceptions of their social responsibilities and evolve courses suited to the many rather than to the college-bound few. But wide experimentation is necessary before teachers can really understand those they teach, before they can enter vicariously into the problems these young people face and help them to acquire the understanding, the insight, the skills, and the social attitudes that will be vital to them in their long out-of-school years.

[1] G. Lester Anderson and T. J. Berning, "What Happens to High School Graduates?" in *Studies of Higher Education*, Biennial Report of the Committee on Educational Research, 1938–40 (Minneapolis: University of Minnesota, 1941), pp. 15–40; Howard M. Bell, *Youth Tell Their Story* (Washington, D. C.: American Council on Education, 1938); Ruth E. Eckert and Thomas O. Marshall, *When Youth Leave School*, Report of the Regents' Inquiry (New York: McGraw-Hill, 1939); Homer P. Rainey, *How Fare American Youth?* (Washington, D. C.: American Council on Education, 1938).

4

THE GENERAL COLLEGE

Bringing well over two thirds of our young people into the high school has of course led to greatly increased attendance in post-secondary institutions, though the expansion has been less impressive than at the high school level. This trend gives every indication of continuing until, as the Educational Policies Commission has suggested, at least half of our young people will remain in school until the age of twenty. In the task of providing appropriate education for these new groups of young people, representing for the most part students with patterns of abilities, interests, and long-range goals not previously served by our colleges, lies a very searching test of education in a democracy. It is never difficult to stimulate superior students to continue their learning and to prepare for the leadership that should be theirs. But is it not possible, and socially, politically, and economically mandatory, to broaden the viewpoints of the vast masses of our people, to open new vistas of interests to them, and to incline them more directly toward social goals? In other words, can American colleges, as well as American secondary schools, evolve appropriate programs of study and work for *average* young people — for the kinds of young people who will be the very backbone or bulwark of American democracy in years to come? In a democratic state decisions must be made by all its citizens, and it is therefore essential that every young person be educated both for intelligent participation in democratic processes and for the personal growth and development that are the goals of our democratic living.

Too often the young people who enter college today find themselves in a welter of confusion, as they are forced to select from a wide array of specialized courses those that may be suited to their individual and special needs. At the University of Minnesota, for example, some six hundred courses are open to freshmen and sophomores, over five hundred of which have been planned largely to suit the requirements of those who will progress to advanced work in particular fields. As President Coffman once pointed out, "Differentiation of the materials of instruction has been carried to such a point that it is practically impossible for a student to receive . . . a general view of any field of human learning. . . . Knowledge has been so attenuated that only fragments and pieces are presented in any course." [2] This atomistic assortment of courses is unfortunate for the student who stays in college only a year or two and for the potential specialist, who ought also to have acquaintance with human conflict and progress and meaning outside the field of his own specialty. No matter how much of a leader he may be in that field he is a follower in all the others.

EXPERIMENTS IN GENERAL EDUCATION

Because the typical liberal arts and junior college curriculums have seemed appropriate neither for the many newcomers to our colleges nor for certain of those young people who would enroll as a matter of course in higher institutions, various new types of offerings have emerged in recent years. By and large these new courses have been designed to prepare young people for their common or general personal, social, and civic responsibilities. The term most frequently used to describe such programs, *general education*, is difficult to define, for general education is characterized not so much by a definitely formulated ideology as by a broad awareness of the need to restore unity and purpose to students' learning. Against the conventional curriculum of the schools — its excessive fragmentation, its tendency toward undue specialization, and its total neglect of many areas of out-of-school living — proponents of general education make their vigorous protest. In an effort to provide the desired organization of learning, many different patterns or varieties of general education have been developed during the last decade. These approaches may perhaps be classified roughly into four categories, each exemplified by an outstanding educational experiment.

The St. John's program. One effort to break down departmental barriers and to emphasize the principle of organization in

[2] In a letter to Dr. Edmund E. Day, July 29, 1936, quoted in "Report on Problems and Progress of the General College, University of Minnesota," June 1938, pp. 2–3.

learning is found in the program offered at St. John's College, where teaching is centered around the classics and the liberal arts and directed toward an understanding of the general ideas that have pervaded the various civilizations of the world. The underlying purpose is to discipline young people's minds, primarily through a critical study of the great books of the human race, in reading, writing, reasoning, and the arts of understanding and communication. This type of program is an attempt to rescue education from what is judged to be a serious deterioration in intellectual and scholastic standards and, as Thayer has said, "to restore as central in general education the abilities to read, to write, to speak, and especially to think." [3]

The University of Chicago program. A belief that the ends of general education can be best achieved by helping the student to master the leading ideas and significant facts in broad areas of knowledge characterizes the University of Chicago college plan. Here the junior college curriculum is planned around five comprehensive fields of knowledge — biological science, physical science, social science, the humanities, and English composition. To obtain a general view of these fields, the student takes inclusive survey courses in each one; the amount of information and understanding he thereby gains is revealed through his performance on searching comprehensive examinations. The goal of the Chicago program is to teach students to think and to think always in terms of the basic facts and generalizations that have emerged from long racial experience.

Bennington and Sarah Lawrence colleges; the Rochester Athenaeum. Certain deep-seated and relatively permanent interests of students provide a base for the type of general education offered in certain other institutions. The organization of studies around a field of special interest characterizes the Bennington and Sarah Lawrence programs. As soon as a girl in either of these colleges discovers some strong, meaningful interest she may devote most of her time and effort to it. Largely through independent reading and tutorial conferences, in which other fields of

[3] V. T. Thayer, "Current Trends in the Development of General Education," *Educational Record*, 20:378–79.

human activity are viewed in relation to this dominant interest, some measure of general education is thereby achieved. Likewise, at the Rochester Athenaeum, where occupational interests are given a central position, cooperative employment serves to supplement, enrich, and vivify the student's school experiences and to throw a searching light on the suitability of his vocational goal. This goal — that of the student's prospective occupation — serves as the initial point of departure, so that breadth in educational experiences is achieved by constantly working outward from the student's underlying occupational motivations.

The Stephens and the General College plan. At Stephens College and at the General College of the University of Minnesota a fourth approach to general education is represented by curriculums organized primarily around certain common human needs. At Stephens College these needs were identified by means of Charters' survey of the everyday activities of three hundred young women who had been graduated from Stephens College. Their most persistent problems, the survey revealed, could be classified in seven major areas — communications, appreciation of the beautiful, social adjustment, physical health, mental health, consumers' problems, and philosophy of living — and around the subject matter suggested by these problems the curriculum was organized. Thus educational experiences have been designed to assist students in acquiring the principles, facts, and skills women ought to possess to live effectively in our present society.

At the General College four such areas of need have been identified, and courses designed to meet them have been set up to supplement the regular subject field offerings. The first orientation area has as its special province personal and individual problems, the second concerns home and family relationships, the third deals with the problems of choosing and adjusting to a vocation, and the fourth area explores those basic contemporary problems that influence each person's thoughts and actions in a democratic society. These areas correspond closely to those outlined by the Educational Policies Commission as the major concerns of education: self-realization, human relationships, economic efficiency, and civic responsibility.

8

THE MEANING OF GENERAL EDUCATION

Although these four approaches to general education differ in many important respects, they also have much in common. Whether the curriculum is of the subject-centered or of the so-called functional-need type, many of the same basic goals are sought in all four. Inherent in them seems to be the agreement that general education, though by no means antithetic to vocational education, is distinguished primarily by the fact that it represents a preparation for the more common responsibilities and privileges of life in a democratic society. The courses included in such programs have been designed to serve both the nonspecialist and the specialist in his general living rather than in his occupational training and pursuits. Back of all these programs is a conviction that intelligent and purposeful behavior must be undergirded by a deep and broad insight into human motivation and achievement. In all these colleges, therefore, the student is stimulated and encouraged in many ways to develop a frame of reference into which particular ideas or events will fit in their proper relations.

In these new syntheses course and departmental barriers are broken down in order to give young people "a sense of life and of education as a living, unified organism, functional and not made up of different blocks of dead matter."[4] Likewise students are challenged to think in terms of living in a democracy — and living not only in terms of holding a job but in terms of personal and family problems and of the broader social aspects of life. Many of the courses organized for general education begin with the known and proceed to the unknown; they start with the geographically and temporally near and progress to the remote. The underlying assumption in several of these programs seems to be that a study of contemporary situations better prepares the student for life and that, properly taught, such courses are as stimulating and productive of intellectual values as the more traditional curriculums.

[4] Malcolm S. MacLean, "A College of 1934," *Journal of Higher Education*, 5:241.

9

OUTCOMES OF GENERAL EDUCATION

The present study represents an evaluation of one of these programs of general education, that offered by the General College at the University of Minnesota. The General College was founded in 1932 in an effort to serve better the many young people who were being dropped from the other divisions of the university or who voluntarily withdrew after only a year or two of college training. Since its establishment ten years ago this program has been offered to approximately a thousand students each year. In at least two ways this two-year curriculum represents a significant pioneering movement in junior college education. In the first place, a deliberate attempt has been made to develop courses that are contemporary and widely useful to students. These new courses attempt to deal not only with the problems young people now face but with those they will undoubtedly encounter after they leave college. In the second place, the General College offers such a program to students whose scholastic ability is just typical of that of high school juniors and seniors. Since few higher institutions have made any deliberate effort to serve such young people, although more and more of them will undoubtedly come to college, the General College venture assumes a special interest. The University of Minnesota has been in a peculiarly advantageous position to experiment in the field of general education because as a state university it attracts students from all levels of ability and possesses unusual resources in staff and equipment. In addition, several General Education Board grants have made it possible to launch critical studies of the problems of general education.

Because of the intrinsic interest of the General College program as well as the wide influence it has already exerted on the general education movement in the United States, careful appraisal of this experiment has seemed essential. The problems which led the University of Minnesota to establish its General College and which have been faced in developing the new program are problems that must unquestionably be encountered by other communities and states as they strive to provide appropriate education for young people of average academic abilities. Certainly it has become increasingly clear that such post-secondary education cannot be assumed by the standard liberal arts college without radically altering its program. Unless far-reaching changes are made in the liberal arts curriculum, our greatly expanded student body will be given many courses for which large numbers of students are obviously unsuited by endowment or interest. On the other hand, if the liberal arts program is changed or modified to provide for these new groups of young people, potential scholars will be robbed of their rightful intellectual challenge and the liberal arts college might easily be still further diverted from its acknowledged mission, the education of scholars. For these reasons it seems important to inquire into the success of a general education program specifically planned for young people who in their backgrounds, interests, abilities, and goals are typical of the vast majority of American high school graduates.

The present volume is a report of a first exploratory attempt to discover what the General College at Minnesota has accomplished and what it may have yet failed to accomplish. Without such an appraisal of the actual outcomes of a new curriculum, for the purpose of organizing school experiences the better to meet young people's requirements, no educational program can be rightly termed experimental.

CHAPTER 2

Evaluation in the General College

Appraisal of the more important outcomes of general education is a difficult but highly challenging task that demands the collective talent and enthusiasm of faculty, administration, and students. The evaluation of a broad educational program can never be the responsibility of one individual, for no single person can possibly collect and adequately appraise the many kinds of evidence necessary for judging its actual worth. A cooperative approach to appraisal has been attempted, and to some degree realized, at the General College. Since a definite philosophy of evaluation has guided the choice of specific procedures and instruments, the point of view underlying the present appraisal deserves rather explicit statement.

WHAT EVALUATION MEANS

During the last few years the new terms *evaluation* and, still more recently, *appraisal* have appeared frequently in discussions of educational problems. These terms appropriately emphasize the importance of planning educational studies, developing ways of measuring outcomes of instruction, and interpreting the results in terms of a fundamental belief concerning the nature and purposes of education. Our whole thinking about educational problems promises to be affected profoundly by the persistent efforts now being made to find out what kinds of changes in students themselves are being brought about by the experiences provided in our schools and colleges. Many teachers have begun to appraise the work that they are accomplishing in their own classrooms, and studies of the outcomes of education in institutions or in entire regions have already yielded challenging results.

Basic to educational evaluation is the point of view that the success of a school or college is most validly judged by examining its students — their understanding and insight, their control of basic skills, the character of the activities in which they participate outside the classroom, their social attitudes, and their goals for the future. We used to make the easy assumption that desirable patterns of living and thinking naturally resulted from the pervasive influence of the objectives of an institution, the skill of the individual teachers, or the content of a textbook. But we are coming to realize more and more that the students themselves are the test of any educational system. Attention has thus been shifted from the *process* to the *product*. It has also become clear that the school's product should be conceived to include all the young people who have had any contact with its program, not merely the graduates. For example, in the case of the General College, the success of the curriculum ought to be judged by alterations that have occurred in the thinking and behavior not only of those students who receive degrees but of the many who drop out of college after a year, or even after one quarter.

In addition to this forthright acknowledgment — that the curriculum as it exists *in students,* and not the formulation of it that exists in teachers' minds or in syllabi or in courses of study, is the ultimate measure of any school's effectiveness — other features tend to distinguish present appraisal studies from many earlier efforts to measure educational outcomes. For instance, no adequate appraisal can be planned until the goals of a particular school or college have been rather explicitly outlined. Evaluation studies rest on the assumption that the school's successes and the school's failures must be viewed in the light of the objectives toward which all its activities have been directed. Outcomes can only be fairly appraised as they are seen to grow out of the strivings and purposings of students, teachers, counselors, administrators, and the whole social order that maintains the school.

Before this first essential step in evaluation is taken — that is, the clarification of goals appropriate to a given institution — studies must usually be made to determine what actually are the needs of its students and the needs of the society in which they live. Only then can differences between the present status of students and the outcomes deemed appropriate for them individually and collectively be clearly identified. At least a first "educated guess" about the nature of these needs must precede evaluation, because it is impossible for an educator to judge the worth of any discovered outcomes without being convinced that one type of growth is more desirable for a given group of students than some other type might be. Every attempt made to find out what a school is accomplishing should help to refine these goals by furnishing clues to the characteristics that students ought to possess to achieve their purposes effectively. The fact that an appraisal should be planned in terms of an institution's basic philosophy does not imply, of course, that the validity of the goals that have been set should not be critically examined from time to time. Rather it emphasizes the fact that educational efforts cannot be intelligently redirected until the value of what the institution is now trying to accomplish is thoroughly understood.

Because an evaluation study depends intimately upon established objectives, it must be specifically planned for a particular institution or school system. Only in this way may the distinctive goals of an institution, as well as those common to other schools or colleges, be properly recognized and appreciated. Certain methods of assessing the understandings, attitudes, and conduct of young people that have been found useful in one institution may be equally helpful in others, but every effort to measure outcomes should be undertaken fully as much to reveal differences in outcomes among schools as to show the attainment of common or basic objectives. No evaluation instrument or device should be isolated from the curriculum of the institution studied, nor should an evaluation program, any more than the curriculum itself, be formulated without considering the characteristics of the young people whom the school serves. Vitally important is this concept of integration in the whole learning process, the concept of the essential unity of a school's philosophy, its curriculum and counseling, and its efforts at self-appraisal. Perhaps this insistence upon the development of an evaluation program in the light of the goals and resources of each particular institution most clearly distinguishes evaluation studies from many earlier surveys in which a common yardstick and common criteria of judgment were applied to great numbers of schools, despite fundamental differences in student potentialities and social opportunities.

By its very nature an evaluation study should be a cooperative undertaking. Instead of having external standards imposed on them, teachers and students must themselves help to define the needs the school or college shall attempt to meet, to clarify goals for their own learning, and to make persistent, imaginative efforts to find out how the school actually affects its students. There is, of course, a distinct place for the expert's specialized help on technical problems, yet at its best the process of evaluation becomes a pervasive point of view, a wholesome questioning as to which educational experiences are really of demonstrable worth to young people. As a result, the whole faculty and the whole student body come to understand better how growth is achieved and thus gain markedly in their ability to give intelligent self-direction to their future efforts. Teachers who have actively entered into the process of evaluation and who have a clear-eyed vision of what their efforts may mean for the everyday thinking and living of young people can no longer either complacently accept tradition or advocate change without critically projecting its consequences. Likewise students who participate in appraising their own work will have a new purposefulness and sense of direction. Careful appraisal also helps to reveal to those outside the classroom the real quality of the school's contribution. It assures educators of a more objective judgment of the whole school program, and so helps to lay the basis for sure-footed, realistic change.

Evaluation studies can hardly be confined to a short period of time, such as a year or two. Instead, appraisal should be a continuing process. The value of the learning experiences provided by a school must be judged in terms of the actual educational outcomes they build; new organizations must then be made to approach more closely the desired goals, and further, more penetrating evaluations must be planned. As long as education is conceived of as a dynamic process, evaluation must contribute to the definition of problems, to the careful consideration of proposed changes, and to the sharper focusing of teaching effort on really important goals. No program can rightly be termed experimental unless provisions are made for such a continuous study of the outcomes of the experiment.

Because appraisal should be an intrinsic part of every learning experience, evaluation studies cannot usually be carried on within a rigidly controlled experimental environment. In other words, the curriculum and the prevailing instructional methods ought not to be "frozen" for the duration of the study. As young people grow and progress in a given field, their competencies need to be appraised and reappraised and so carefully defined that what they can do at various points in their growth will be unmistakably clear both to the young people themselves and to teachers, parents, and prospective employers. In an appraisal study, therefore, one must first of all find out what is happening to young people *under ordinary school conditions* instead of in some artificially created experimental situation. Occasionally rigid controls are essential to isolate the factors that produce a given outcome, but extensive day-by-day observations and measurements will provide the most convincing evidence of what a particular school is doing and what it is still failing to do.

In any evaluation study a great many evidences of growth or change must be gathered and carefully weighed. Ideally the exploration of changes in young people's thinking and living should be as extensive as the desired outcomes. Any direction in which young people may be expected to develop as a result of spending their years in a selected school environment, rather than completing the process of maturation in some other way, should be a matter of concern to the evaluator. Instead of viewing some limited aspect of student life or of confining observation and measurement to some single, isolated variable, he must inquire into many aspects of growth involving physical, intellectual, emotional, and social development. He must marshal his evidence from the painstaking observations of those who know young people well, from carefully formulated tests of aptitude, interest, and attitude, from young people's own estimates of their strengths and weaknesses and of their hopes and plans for the future, and from all the varied activities in which they engage, both inside and outside the school. One distinct advantage in considering many different types of evidence is that they serve as checks on one another, partially compensating for the subjective and variable clues furnished by any of these indicators considered singly. A variety of outcomes must also be explored because the needs of the world in which students live and certainly the needs of any one individual are not all of one kind. No one measure of excellence, such as ability to succeed in academic situations, can yield an adequate evaluation of a school program. Only through persistent scouting for many types of talent will adequate recognition be given to individuality or to those distinctive strengths and weaknesses on which each person's progress must depend.

The total patterning of the characteristics young people show when they leave school or complete a program is often of far greater significance in appraising the worth of that program than is their development in any single direction. This emphasis on interrelationships and reinforcements among traits, as well as on the sheer amount of growth, still further complicates the task of evaluation. It means that results from no single test or battery of tests will adequately demonstrate the values of the program but that much reliance must be placed on the mature, comprehensive judgment of those intimately acquainted with all the evidences. An appraisal of a school program will be satisfactory only if it utilizes all relevant information, all the specific, concrete data that may be gathered about students and about social needs, and if, in addition, the judgments based on these evidences are arrived at cooperatively, embodying the thinking of students, teachers, and others not directly connected with the school.

Despite their much greater complexity evaluation studies ought to be in no sense less rigorous from a statistical standpoint than are investigations based primarily on the study and analysis of single variables. The more varied the kinds of evidence we collect in studies of educational outcomes, the greater the need to know the validity and reliability of these measures, the greater the ingenuity demanded in evolving an appropriate experimental design, and the greater the skill exacted in drawing reasonable generalizations from all these evidences. Moreover, efforts to trace the growth of students over a period of years and to study many aspects of human talent must always require the most refined analytical techniques. Unceasing efforts must be made to describe, and to measure with increasing precision, every change in young people that gives promise of leading to their more competent participation in activities appropriate to them individually. Because appraisal studies emphasize interrelationships, because they try to view simultaneously and steadily a young person's successes both in the classroom and in out-of-school situations, they require thorough technical competence in the analysis of basic data. Even more, they demand what may be termed a statistical conscience in interpreting results.

Finally, the very term *evaluation* implies that an entirely frank accounting be made of the findings of the study. Both the school's successes and the school's failures should be thoughtfully presented. Too often in educational studies attention is focused only on the strengths of a program, on what it has meant to the young people who have really succeeded in it. Teachers who try to embody certain features of that program in a new setting are thus often discouraged because of unforeseen difficulties or unexpected obstacles. The evidence indicating that certain goals have not been reached should be as clearly identified and as thoughtfully analyzed as the evidence of positive contributions. Only in this way can school programs be constructively improved.

EARLIER STUDIES OF THE GENERAL COLLEGE PROGRAM

The studies reported in this volume summarize what is now known about the effectiveness of the General College program. On no single count have these investigations met the criteria outlined above, for the evidence available at present certainly does not answer unequivocally the basic question of whether or not General College young people are more generally competent than those trained in a traditional college program. Only a crude beginning has been made in the direction of actual appraisal — a preliminary view that suggests both the tremendous difficulties of evaluating a broad-gauged program and the compelling challenge that such a task offers for the staff of any school. Although these attempts to test the worth of some aspects of one institutional program have yielded few definite answers, they have deepened the conviction that in cooperative, penetrating, and unceasing appraisal lies one of the surest hopes for education in a democracy. Clear improvement can only come when the needs of young people and of our society are known and when procedures are continuously refined to insure free, vigorous personal and social growth.

Much spadework had been accomplished before this two-year evaluation study was begun in the General College in September 1938.[1] An important first step was the development of an experimental attitude on the part of the faculty — a willingness to weigh alternative proposals, to try new approaches, and to face honestly the results of these curriculum ventures. When the college was established the idea of general education was new to the instructors, most of whom had either recently graduated from specialized programs of study or held academic rank in some other division of the university. The students they were to serve differed markedly in academic ability from their own college associates or their former students in other colleges, and there were few charts to guide the exploration. Yet almost from the beginning faculty members sought to parallel the development of new curriculum materials and teaching procedures with attempts to test their "educated guesses" concerning the needs of youth and the responsibilities of the college for meeting them.

Two broadly descriptive studies were launched during this period. The first surveyed the abilities, interests, attitudes, and family backgrounds of the young people then enrolled in the General College,[2] and the second probed the major problems, activities, and needs of young adults who had attended the University of Minnesota.[3] These investigations were not intended to

[1] A grant from the General Education Board of the Rockefeller Foundation, which also sponsored the college's personnel and curriculum studies, provided most of the funds for this evaluation study.

[2] Cornelia T. Williams, *These We Teach* (Minneapolis: University of Minnesota Press, 1943).

[3] C. Robert Pace, *They Went to College* (Minneapolis: University of Minnesota Press, 1941).

demonstrate what the General College program itself had contributed to effective out-of-school living, yet the findings assisted materially in charting the areas in which later studies might be made to test the outcomes of the program. In addition, during the six-year period before the present evaluation was initiated, the entire faculty had given much attention to the development of broad-gauged examinations, both for particular courses and for comprehensive areas. This test-building not only supplied valuable items for the construction of new examinations but served to educate the whole staff in the point of view and methods of evaluation.[4]

Certain positive and more specific discoveries concerning the worth of the General College program emerged from studies made during these early years. Brown's studies, for example, revealed that young people who had taken the General College nonlaboratory human biology or physical science courses, when compared with other students of equal ability who had taken the usual prerequisite courses in zoology and chemistry, were under no handicap in their sequent science courses in the College of Agriculture, Forestry, and Home Economics.[5] Eurich's preliminary study of the records of General College students who transferred to other divisions of the university likewise indicated that in their subsequent university work they fared as well as other students of similar academic promise.[6] In two other investigations, one in current affairs courses and the other in the biological sciences, the same tests were administered to General College students and to outside control groups. Again it appeared that when adjustments were made for differences in initial ability General College students gained as much in information, breadth of understanding, and the ability to apply their knowledge as

[4] Alvin C. Eurich and Palmer O. Johnson, "The Experimental Examination in the General College," Chap. III in *The Effective General College Curriculum as Revealed by Examinations* (Minneapolis: University of Minnesota Press, 1937).
[5] Clara Brown, *A Study of Prerequisite Sciences and Certain Sequent Courses at the University of Minnesota* (Minneapolis: University of Minnesota, Committee on Educational Research, 1941).
[6] Alvin C. Eurich, "A Study of Subsequent Academic Achievement of General College Transfer Students," Chap. XIII in *The Effective General College Curriculum*, pp. 303-7.

young people in other divisions of the university.[7] These earlier researches, in other words, suggest no academic handicap from General College attendance. They do not indicate, of course, in what respects the outcomes of the new program may be superior or inferior to those of the typical liberal arts curriculum.

THE SCOPE OF THIS STUDY

In the special two-year evaluation discussed in this book, the results of earlier studies have been coordinated and interpreted and new studies have been launched to fill in blind spots in the existing evidences. The following brief outline of basic questions investigated during this period suggests the problems at which these new researches were aimed.

A first necessary task was to identify and render as explicit as possible the goals of the General College program, so that appraisal might be focused on objectives judged important by those actually responsible for the curriculum. Although during the two years of this appraisal study the development of a detailed statement of goals was only begun, even a tentative statement assisted immeasurably in judging the importance of the various changes discovered during and after the students' residence in the General College. In addition, tentative statements of objectives were also formulated for the divisional areas so that particular courses and sequences might be viewed in the light of their special contributions to the total program.

Another major task, on which much more progress can be reported, was to obtain a clear description of General College students. It seemed important not only to find out what kinds of young people were enrolled in the college but also to inquire into the types of programs they selected, their success in meeting the scholastic requirements of the college, and the length of time they remained at the university. The so-called adolescent study, which was begun in 1935 and reported in another volume in this series, has revealed many facts about the abilities of General Col-

[7] Alvin C. Eurich, Edgar Weaver, and Elmo C. Wilson, "Contemporary Affairs Studies," Chap. IV, and Palmer O. Johnson, "Biological Science Studies," Chap. XI, in *The Effective General College Curriculum.*

lege students, their home backgrounds, their leisure-time and vocational interests, and their plans for the future.[8] Studies reported in Chapters 4 and 5, below, show the extent to which these particular traits are characteristic of the students now enrolled in the General College. In addition, the relation of certain of these traits to success in the General College program has been analyzed, so that some clues have been discovered concerning the kinds of students who are most adequately served by this particular program.

A third important undertaking, which was the major concern of the present study and which offered far greater difficulties, has been to explore the specific character of the changes that occur in young people as they progress through the General College. For example, do students become better informed, more enlightened in their attitudes, and more competent in dealing with personal and social problems as they continue their work in the college? Do they tend to engage in more leisure-time activities or in different types of activities? Do they develop more constructive, realistic plans for the future? Obtaining evidences on some of these points has been extremely difficult, for although social competence may be the chief goal of all the experiences provided by the General College, direct measurement of behavior in out-of-school situations could not be made within the resources of this study. Instead, a few of the many factors that may contribute to social competence have been carefully examined. Measures of skills, information, attitudes, and educational and social adjustment have provided a partial basis for evaluation. The immediate and long-range objectives expressed by young people just before leaving college offer another test of the character of the guidance and instruction they had received. Though only exploratory studies could be made within the time available, the results suggest some notably successful aspects of the program and some aspects in which hopes have not yet been realized.

A fourth significant question pertains to the attitudes of students and faculty members toward the General College program.

[8] Williams, *These We Teach*.

22

What do students enrolled in the college judge to be the chief assets and chief liabilities of this general education program? What types of courses do they believe have been most helpful to them individually? Least helpful to them? What values do they attach to counseling? What new offerings or new services would they like to see incorporated in the program? How ready would they be to reenter the General College themselves or to recommend the program to a younger brother or sister? What do faculty members see as the major strengths and weaknesses of the General College curriculum? Of course, the opinions of students and faculty can provide only a partial basis for appraisal, yet these subjective reactions have intrinsic interest and value because they reveal the impact of the program on those most intimately concerned with it.

A final and more crucial test of the worth of the General College program lies in the postcollege careers of its students — both those who withdraw from college and those who are graduated. Of those who transfer to other divisions of the university, what proportions complete the programs of their choice? And with what success? Of those who leave school to go to work, how many find jobs, and what sorts of jobs are they? How satisfied do they appear to be with the vocational adjustments they have made and with the preparation that the General College has given them to meet these oncoming work responsibilities? Are their home and family relationships noticeably happier than those of students who left the university before the General College was established? What differences appear between General College students and those in other colleges with respect to their enjoyment of leisure time, participation in community activities, and allegiance to the basic tenets of American democracy? Three studies, involving young people who dropped out of the General College over a period of two years, students who transferred during the same period to other divisions of the university, and students (both those who dropped out and those who graduated) who had been out of school from three to seven years, provide revealing evidences of the residual outcomes of this program.

OUTCOMES OF GENERAL EDUCATION

Attaining the goal they had set for themselves — that of a thorough evaluation of the General College program — was a difficult task for the evaluation staff and the faculty, and the results naturally fell short of what they had hoped for. One of the most baffling obstacles was, and continues to be, the lack of appropriate measuring instruments. It is true that many colleges and research centers have attempted for years to develop examinations that probe abilities to generalize, to appraise evidences, and to make meaningful applications of materials that have been learned, as well as to assess the basic understandings and insights upon which these must rest. Yet the successful construction of such instruments has in fact only begun. Even less success has attended efforts to measure outcomes that cannot be fully appraised by paper-and-pencil tests. Promising starts have indeed been made in exploring attitudes, motivations, and appreciations, but a great many new instruments and observational techniques must be perfected before the significance of any experimental curriculum can be fully assayed.

Still another highly disturbing problem in carrying out such a study lies in the fact that uniformity of outcomes among students is to be neither expected nor desired. However broad may be our concept of the well-adjusted individual (a man or woman, for example, who is eager and able to participate vigorously in the life about him), we cannot draw up a standard description of a generally educated person that we can use in judging whether a college has actually filled the needs of each one of its students. Young people differ almost inconceivably in their abilities and interests, their home backgrounds and school experiences, their present outlooks and future intentions, so that what constitutes readiness for new responsibilities for one young person may really be very imperfect preparation for another. The criterion that ought to be used, given the appropriate resources, is that of relevancy, or the pertinence of school or college experiences to the special and individual needs of each student. All the collected evidences ought to be analyzed to show the pattern of each person's development and the extent to which he has learned things he most needed to learn for rich, continuous growth. In the present study, however, only a few of the more common needs of students could be identified — needs related to the educational, social, and vocational adjustments that practically all students must some day make.

Several formidable difficulties were inherent in the local situation at this university. One persistent problem was the severe limitation of the resources available for making such a study. Determining the impact of a program on young people requires extensive investigation of what students are actually thinking and doing. Many pre- and post-tests within the school, careful observations of learning activities in the classroom, surveys of student life on the campus, interviews with young people, their parents, and employers outside the school — all these must be considered if the goal is a comprehensive appraisal. The staff of the present study consisted of only one full-time director for the two-year period and two half-time assistants. Most of the actual tabulation and analysis, therefore, had to be done by students on NYA appointments and by WPA workers. As a result it was necessary to limit sharply the outcomes to be explored. Furthermore even if a larger technical staff had been available, the gathering and interpretation of the materials would have required far more time than faculty and students could give to the project. The overworked faculty of the college, handling classes in which the enrollment usually reaches a hundred, and most of them carrying more than a full teaching and counseling load, can hardly supply the detailed information concerning individual students that members of a small college staff can so easily provide. For this reason, requests for faculty assistance were restricted to critical problems that could not be studied without it. The administrative and instructional staffs, however, were intensely interested in the study, and the many invaluable contributions they made served to indicate how much the evaluation might have been broadened and deepened if more faculty time had been available.

Similar obstacles were encountered in obtaining student cooperation. For example, the fact that typical students remain in the college only one year made it extremely difficult to enlist their

25

aid in planning and carrying through the study. Nevertheless they did contribute substantially to some of the projects.

A college established for students of lesser scholastic ability also finds itself faced with a serious morale problem — the revolt of many young people against a program they have not voluntarily elected. All the resentment that youth may feel toward inappropriate courses taken in secondary schools or colleges elsewhere, toward ill-advised counseling or a total lack of counseling in their previous school careers, or toward the hard fact of their own inability to master a more or less set pattern of advanced academic courses may easily be vented on the one college in which they are permitted to enroll. Serious disaffection does not characterize all General College students, or even the majority; some come voluntarily, and a great many others modify their attitudes after a few weeks' or months' residence in the college. But evaluation must begin under a strong handicap when many students are somewhat suspicious of this general education program and of efforts to determine its outcomes.

Difficulties that arise from the initial attitudes of many students toward the college are intensified by the fact that the majority of the students remain in the General College for a much shorter time than students do in other colleges of the university. This brief attendance may be in itself an important fact in appraising the General College program, but the significance of even the best program cannot be accurately judged when many students do not remain long enough to permit the faculty to identify their individual problems and to familiarize them with the varied resources that the college can offer for meeting their needs.

Another subtle but none the less serious difficulty lies in the lack of prestige of the General College in the eyes of many people outside the college. The struggle that an experimental program always encounters in winning a place for itself among traditional and established programs is not new in educational history. General College experience only repeats what vocational schools and colleges of home economics, agriculture, or education — to select only a few of the competitors of the classical curriculum — have faced again and again. The General College situation, however, is accentuated by the fact that 80 per cent of its students come by definite assignment rather than by voluntary choice. Efforts to organize an educational program directed toward quite different types of goals may easily be devaluated by those who know only one criterion of school accomplishment — ability to succeed in book learning. There must be a much longer period of education for both faculty and students in the university and for members of the community at large before this experiment in general education will have had a really fair opportunity to demonstrate its intrinsic strengths and weaknesses.

The present report is therefore frankly exploratory in nature. It attempts to clarify a few major issues in general education and to present whatever data are now available concerning the worth of the general education program offered at Minnesota. Through a complete sharing of results it may be possible to conserve for secondary and higher education elsewhere the more significant outcomes of the experimental attack made by the faculty and administration of Minnesota's General College on the problem of education for vigorous, effective living.

CHAPTER 3

Objectives of the General College

Evaluation studies should be conceived and developed in terms of the goals that a particular institution has set for itself. The pertinence of these objectives to the students in the college and to the social order in which the college functions should of course be vigorously questioned; for the goals themselves are as legitimate a province for evaluation as are the procedures and techniques employed in an effort to realize them. There is first of all an obligation, however, to find out how well the college is achieving what it believes to be its major purposes. The extent to which teachers' and students' objectives for the program as a whole have been realized in the thinking and behavior of the students themselves is the crucial test of any educational institution.

With the basic philosophy or point of view of the General College, most faculty members have been well acquainted from the first. The very process of developing new courses has helped them to clarify the concept of general education. The nation-wide attention, both in approval and attack, that the General College program attracted has also meant that faculty members have been far more articulate than the usual college staff concerning the major purposes of the college. Yet when the present appraisal studies began there existed no detailed statement of the goals of the program. Objectives had been formulated mainly for separate courses or for divisional areas. Frequently these statements had been prepared by instructors or examination assistants as a kind of blueprint to assist them in constructing course or comprehensive examinations. Instructors in one field often had not seen the statements formulated by members in other fields, and thus there was no general formulation to show explicitly how their various teaching efforts were interrelated.

OBJECTIVES OF THE GENERAL COLLEGE

Because such a generally accepted outline of goals was essential to give direction to the evaluation, one of the first steps in the present study was the development of such a statement. For this purpose a committee on General College objectives was appointed by the director of the college in October 1938. The committee consisted of two teaching members, a counselor, the director of curriculum revision, the director of the college, and the evaluator.

This committee decided to ask all members of the teaching staff and a few other persons closely associated with the General College program to contribute short statements of what they considered to be the chief aims of the college. These ideas were to be expressed in terms of the thinking and behavior of the students and were to emphasize particularly those understandings, abilities, and attitudes that the faculty hoped a young person might possess at the end of his General College residence. More specifically they were to constitute each person's best present answer to the question "What do you think a General College student should be like after spending two years in this college?" This approach was explained to each faculty member individually, to gain his cooperation.

The vigorous response gave evidence of real interest in the clarification of the basic objectives of the college. Every full-time faculty member of the college prepared a description of a "generally educated" young person, as did most of their colleagues from other colleges who did some teaching in the General College and had hence been invited to share in this project. Forty statements were received, representing all departments of instruction, the counseling division, and the administration.

These descriptions were exceedingly interesting human documents, showing rather vividly the directions in which the Minnesota concept of general education had been developing. As illustrative of the kinds of materials from which a general statement was finally evolved, three of the replies are reproduced in full.

OUTCOMES OF GENERAL EDUCATION

THE GENERAL COLLEGE GRADUATE

Those who are products of general education realize that their education is not finished at the end of two years in college but that it is a life process. They not only realize it but continue to grow throughout their lives. Thus the following characteristics will not be fully matured at the end of two years' education but will be in the process of development during the two years (many of them before that time) and will continue throughout their adult lives:

They are aware of their own limitations but at the same time constantly realize and develop their talents, whatever they may be. Likewise they appreciate and encourage the varying abilities and talents of their fellows, recognizing and respecting qualities of leadership as well as the particular services of those who play more humble roles. (This applies to themselves as well as to the other fellow.) They are persons of good taste and discernment. They respect intellectual attainments, though they themselves are not necessarily intellectual. They are critically minded, not for the sake of mental exercise but because they know that the ever-present problem of making choices requires the weighing of all available evidence. They are critically minded not only in reading, listening to speeches, or participating in political activities but in furnishing their homes, obtaining medical care, and buying groceries or a pair of shoes. They are actively tolerant, with a tolerance for the immediate as well as the remote. However, they are not complacent but have a passionate hatred of injustice. In them the quality of "divine discontent" is strong. Their understanding of their own personalities and of their relationship to others is being constantly extended. Marriage and family life are important to them, and they look upon them as real jobs, not as a story-book romance. (But let not the atmosphere be too clinical!) They have an alert sense of social responsibility, resulting from their realization of the significance of the individual in a democratic society.

AND I AM TWO-AND-TWENTY

Dear Diary:

It's June 1940. Think of it! Two years ago 1940 seemed about as remote as the year 2,000, and now it is actually here. Time is a funny thing. When life is interesting, events whisk by as if they were part of a fifteen-minute newsreel. The first thing you know the show is over and you're standing outside and for just a minute the people and the buildings and the cars in the street seem a little strange. That's the way I feel now. Graduation is over, I have my Associate in Arts degree, and I can hardly realize that probably I shall never again walk into Wesbrook Hall and fill out a registration blank.

When I entered the university, I thought I wanted four years of college, but now I'm glad I took a two-year course. A profession is not for me. I think I know now what I want to do, and I think I can do it. I had a chance to try myself out at it last summer. Mr. Brown has promised me a permanent job in the cost department the next time he has an opening. The salary isn't large, but there will be opportunities for advancement later on. Of course, money isn't everything. I once thought it was, but now I realize that it's much more important to have the satisfaction of doing well a job for which one is fitted than it is to earn five or ten thousand dollars a year. I know that I will enjoy working with Mr. Brown, and, what is more, I'll have enough free time so that I'll be able to work in my dark room and have an occasional round of golf.

Many things have happened to me during the last few years, but I think that the most important of all is that I have got acquainted with myself. I used to think that the world was my oyster and that all I had to do was crack it. I know now that I'm not quite strong enough to crack it. After all, I guess I'm just an average sort of person. There are some things that I can do better than other people, but most of the time I'm just holding my own. If I have any edge over the other fellow, it's probably that I know my own capabilities and limitations. I know that I have more clerical ability than the average but that I'll probably never paint a picture or write a book. I know I am in most respects a pretty healthy specimen, but I must stay out of competitive sports because of a functional disorder in the activity of my heart. I know I am quick-tempered and a little moody, but I believe I am learning to control my temper and my moods. I think I have learned to eat, to dress, to write, and to talk in a fairly intelligent manner. I know what I like — in houses, in interior decoration, in pictures, in radio programs, and in people; in other words, I think I have acquired some standards of taste.

As I look back over my own personal newsreel, I can't help thinking that I have taken a big step toward becoming grown-up. I have learned to look at myself and other people and events objectively. I have learned that I as an individual am a relatively unimportant element in a very complex world. When I was a child I used to sit on our back steps and watch the ants depositing grains of sand in little doughnut-shaped rings. I remember that though once in a while one of them would get stepped on by the grocery boy or the milk man, the other ants just went right ahead carrying grains of sand. If I should get stepped on, the world won't come to an end. I

31

have learned that my own life is inextricably bound up with that of others and that there are social laws and requisites which I cannot ignore. I know it is my duty not only to vote but to vote for candidates regarding whose qualifications I am well informed. I believe that since one third of the nation is ill-housed, ill-clothed, and ill-fed, there is need for some really effective social legislation in this country. I believe that what is happening in China at the moment may be as important to me as what is happening in Minneapolis or St. Paul. I know *how little I know* — and how much there is to learn. I know what R. L. Stevenson meant by "The world is so full of a number of things," and knowing that, I believe life is worth living.

A DESCRIPTION OF A GENERALLY EDUCATED YOUNG PERSON

He has become increasingly aware of his individual and special needs, his particular strengths, and his more important limitations, so that he appreciates his uniqueness and is motivated to make his own best contributions of skill and talent. In addition he recognizes, and takes into account in his planning, human variability and the wide range of individual differences existing among other people.

He has become more clearly oriented in his physical and social world, understanding the conditioning background of many present problems and their implications for human living.

He has attained sufficient command of the basic skills and techniques of social communication, a fund of important information and understandings, and a deepened curiosity concerning his world that fit him for continued study and learning, either in schools or in the everyday contacts of adult life.

He is ready to play an active part in the world's work, possessing a vocational goal that is reasonable in terms of both individual and social needs. He also knows where he can obtain specialized training and understands specifically how to attack the problems of getting and holding a job in his own community.

He is prepared and motivated to participate intelligently, honestly, and sensibly in the formal duties of citizenship and in the informal activities of his family and community.

His affective experience is being continuously widened and deepened in tone, so that he derives keen enjoyment from the sensory world about him and from human relationships. Continuing interests and hobbies have been built up that will enrich his out-of-school living by providing emotional release and self-expression.

He is in the process of developing and applying increasingly valid standards of appraisal, with the result that he attempts to select his vocational, home-life, and free-time activities in such a way that they contribute to his own growth and also render him a more effective husband, father, worker, friend, and citizen.

He has made progress in working out a philosophy of life that is personally satisfying and that shows tolerance, fair-mindedness, and an active concern for the well-being of others.

He is learning to use intelligently the opinions and advice of the expert and yet to assume squarely the responsibility for his own decisions and his own actions, applying his initiative and insight to the issues that confront him and taking the full consequences of his behavior. In other words he has made a hopeful start toward standing on his own feet.

As a first step in formulating a general statement of goals, all the descriptive materials received from the staff were classified under certain major headings. These descriptive statements might have been organized in a number of ways: according to the four so-called functional-need, or life-activity, areas of the General College program — individual orientation, home life orientation, vocational orientation, and socio-civic orientation, according to the divisional subject areas within the college, or according to the types of student behavior involved, such as understandings, skills, attitudes, and interests. The latter plan was finally adopted, since it stressed the fact that the real outcomes of any program are to be discovered in the changes in young people themselves, those fundamental modifications in thinking and behavior that contribute to greater competence in and out of school. The scheme that was followed in this preliminary classification is set forth below.

I. Knowledge as insight and understanding
   A. Concerning personal traits and behavior
   B. Concerning other people
   C. Concerning the physical and social order
II. Skills and abilities
   A. General skills or abilities
   B. Study skills or those basic to communication
   C. Skills involved in thinking
   D. Social skills or abilities
   E. Skills relating to personal development and home maintenance
   F. Skills relating to vocations

III. Attitudes, interests, and appreciations
    A. Scientific or objective approach to problems
    B. Curiosity
    C. Attitudes toward other people
    D. Attitudes toward one's self
    E. Attitudes and interests related to leisure time
IV. Character of the individual's world view
    A. Standards of judgment
    B. Responsibility for action

In this first tentative classification of all the materials submitted by faculty members, the exact language used in each description was retained. Although certain characteristics of students had not been clearly or happily expressed, the members of the committee preferred not to modify the original statements until the whole faculty had had an opportunity to survey and appraise their own efforts in setting forth the philosophy of the college. The plan of classifying every item contributed by the staff obviously resulted in a great deal of overlapping and duplication, so that this first draft consisted of eighteen single-spaced mimeographed pages. Illustrative statements from the first subdivision are reproduced below to show how these descriptive materials, taken from the faculty statements, were marshaled under certain major headings.

I. Knowledge as insight and understanding
    A. Concerning himself
      "He has become increasingly aware of his individual and special needs, his particular strengths, and his more important limitations."
      "He has developed a clearer picture of his abilities and his limitations and has developed an appropriate outlook on life in terms of that picture."
      "He is aware of his own limitations, but at the same time constantly realizes and develops his talents, whatever they may be."
      "He is an individual who knows how little he knows – how much there is to learn."
      "After all, he knows he is just an average sort of person. There are some things he can do better than other people, but most of the time he is just holding his own."
      "He has missed some things that people used to think essen-

tial. But those things he is leaving to professional people. He has discovered his limitations and the limitations of hundreds of thousands of people like himself, and he is willing to leave specialized lives and preliminary specialized types of training to other people, people better equipped for certain types of life."

"He will be convinced of his ability to attain ends which are realistically within his grasp."

"He knows his interests — relatively permanent and relatively transitory interests, discovered partly from relationships with a wide variety of materials and experiences — literature, art, music, science, etc."

"He knows his needs — both immediate and future — partly through orientation courses and through the development of a philosophy."

"He should know his psychological and physical characteristics well enough to take advantage of good traits, bolster weak ones, and compensate for missing ones."

"He will have a sufficient knowledge of himself, of 'the normal,' and of methods of social catharsis to rid himself of abnormal emotional reactions."

"He has a fairly clear picture of his duties and responsibilities as a citizen, worker, member of a family, and as a member of the human race."

"He possesses a reasonable vocational goal and knows where he can obtain specialized training. In addition, he understands specifically how to attack the problems of getting and holding a job in his own community."

"He is wisely oriented toward his job — knows that no psychiatrist or course in personal adjustment can take the place of profitable, enjoyable labor."

While repetitive statements did not contribute to a succinct formulation of General College goals, the reproduction of all the submitted materials made it possible for each faculty member to see the extent to which his own views coincided with or diverged from those of his colleagues. In other words, this first draft revealed sharply certain commonly accepted goals of this general education program as well as other goals that were upheld by small minority groups.

This first draft was then sent to the same General College faculty members and their university colleagues who had been initially invited to participate. An accompanying letter thanked them for their cooperation and outlined what the committee had decided might be a feasible next step in reaching a working statement of goals. The following suggestions were given for the examination of this first tentative draft of objectives:

Because a certain outcome has been specified by one faculty member or by the majority, it may not necessarily be a valid outcome of a program of general education. The importance of these goals must be appraised, taking into consideration not only social needs but also the characteristics of our students and the time available for effecting these changes in thinking and behavior. Because of your active interest in the General College, the committee is therefore asking your cooperation in preparing a more satisfactory and concise statement of our objectives, whether or not you contributed to this first statement.

1. Please check through the list, placing a plus sign (+) in front of each phrase or statement that seems to you to be a legitimate goal of a two-year general college, a question mark (?) in front of those concerning which you have some doubt, and a minus sign (—) prefacing those that you do not consider either valid or feasible objectives for this unit of the university. A few items will probably stand out as being particularly serviceable statements — these may be indicated with a double plus (++).

2. The present classification is admittedly a very tentative one; therefore the committee would be glad to receive any criticisms of organization or of the classification of individual items. Since this mimeographed statement is to be returned to the committee, any notations that you may place in the margins will be carefully noted in making revisions.

3. You may also wish to comment on the general emphasis revealed in this first statement, for certain points may be understressed and others definitely overstressed. Any notations of blind spots will be especially helpful to the committee.

Replies were received from thirty persons out of the original forty-five, the intervention of Christmas holidays being chiefly responsible for reduced participation. Again all major divisions of the college program were adequately represented. To determine the extent of agreement of faculty members with the descriptive statements, opinions were weighted in the following fashion:

OBJECTIVES OF THE GENERAL COLLEGE

Symbol	Attitude	Rating
++	Strong agreement	+2
+	Agreement...................	+1
Blank	No expressed attitude.........	0
?	Goal questioned	−1
—	Disagreement	−2

The thirty judges used in this analysis most frequently endorsed the following statements:

"He has become increasingly aware of his individual and special needs, his particular strengths, and his more important limitations."

"He should have an awareness of current problems and a growing responsibility toward meeting them."

"He has a working knowledge of home and family life, so that he is aware of, and thus better equipped to meet, such problems as those occurring in marital relationships, family finance, and child raising."

"He has a deepened curiosity concerning his world that leads him to continue his learning outside the school."

"He is motivated to participate intelligently, honestly, and sensibly in his family and in broader civic duties."

"He is able to continue his learning in unsupervised situations."

"His capacities for self-expression will be better developed than before his general education."

"He assumes squarely the responsibility for his own decisions and his own actions, applying his initiative and insights to the issues that confront him and taking full consequences for his behavior. He has made a hopeful start toward standing on his own feet."

The least acceptable statements, as judged by these replies, were the following:

"He has come to realize that a profession is not for him."

"He is looking for a job, but not the one he would have looked for two years ago."

"In the majority of cases these young people will be satisfied with mediocrity in later life."

"He will be sure that he knows what he wants out of life."

"After all, he knows that he is just an average sort of person. There are some things he can do better than other people, but most of the time he is just holding his own."

"He plays life's games not in brutal competition but as a good sport, not caring whether he wins, loses, or ties."

The free comments and the hundreds of alterations suggested

37

in the wording of individual items, as well as the ratings given specific statements, helped to clarify faculty attitudes toward this first formulation. The following summary suggests the general tenor of these reactions:

1. Statements should outline goals for *this* general college, not for any two-year institution. Many are goals for the whole educational process, not focused sufficiently on what may be accomplished with *our resources* and *our student body*. Some of these objectives should be handled earlier, and probably by other agencies.

2. Most of these objectives are discouragingly ambitious; there is a need for simpler, less multiple, more concrete statements. Illustrative of this type of criticism are the following comments, which appeared with disturbing frequency throughout the blank — "platitudinous," "utopian," "too much for two years," "four-year grads can't do these things," "can we even make a dent in these directions?"

3. These statements should be toned down to take aptitudes into account, so that realistic consideration will be given to the actual abilities of General College students. Instead of saying, for example, that the individual who has completed his general education "attacks problems with intelligence," it might be better to say that he "attacks them with what intelligence he has."

4. A great many of the statements are vague and too abstract to be useful. Illustrative of faculty attitudes on this point are the following comments: "Beautiful, rich prose, but what does it mean?" "Deucedly general." "How concrete, how Anglo-Saxon!" "Useless as a statement of working objectives."

5. Most objectives are not stated in a sufficiently quantitative manner. Since growth is a matter of degree, this fact should be indicated. The critical issue is how much more General College students will possess these characteristics at the close of their training than at its inception. Too many of the goals are stated in terms of accomplishment.

6. Certain statements suggest that the generally educated person is a pretty complacent individual, easily satisfied with things as they are. At times they even give the impression of the playboy attitude! Others assume that education can be broad without being deep in at least a few spots — outlining a kind of "stratospheric intellectualism."

7. A few of the statements concern *means*, not goals. This is especially true of those given under vocational abilities.

8. Nearly all the aims are probably desirable, but student out-

comes will be affected fully as much by the processes used in their attainment as by the character of the objectives themselves. It is on the question of procedures that the sharpest divisions of opinion may come.

The committee then attempted to eliminate duplication and to simplify the organization and wording of these materials. They also added a few completely new items to fill in the discovered blind spots.

As an indication of the character of these revisions, the section given above, dealing with desired insights into personal traits and behavior, is reproduced in its revised form. This new formulation, which represented a reduction of the original materials from eighteen to seven pages, was then circulated to the faculty for further discussion and for reference in planning instruction.

I. Knowledge as insight and understanding
   A. In coming to know himself he has become increasingly aware of
      1. His individual and special needs, both immediate and future
      2. His interests, both the relatively transitory and the more permanent ones
      3. His strengths — those traits that constitute his greatest assets
      4. His limitations — deficiencies and differences from other people that should affect his job choice and his social adjustments
      5. His motives and long-time goals
      6. His relationships to others, including his opportunities and responsibilities as a parent, citizen, worker, and member of the human race
      7. The meaning of his own pattern of abilities in terms of eventual vocational adjustment
      8. The extent to which his problems are usual and normal
      9. The vast amount that there is to learn, beyond what he himself knows

Discussion of General College objectives has progressed in several directions since this first revision was made. In addition to the more detailed formulation, a brief statement of goals seemed essential, since many people would not take the time to study a lengthy outline. Also, further examinations of the revised draft indicated that certain items were ambiguous or repetitious. One of the first of the committee's tasks the following year (1939–40), therefore, was to prepare such an abbreviated working statement. Because this represents a comprehensive outline of General College goals it is reproduced in full.

OBJECTIVES OF THE GENERAL COLLEGE

I. Knowledge as insight and understanding
  A. In coming to know himself
    1. He has become increasingly aware of his needs, immediate and future, his interests, the relatively transitory and the more permanent ones, his strengths and weaknesses, which should affect his motives and long-time goals
    2. He has grown in the understanding of his relationships to others, including his responsibilities as a member of a family, a community, a work group, and the human race
    3. He understands more fully the meaning of his own pattern of abilities in terms of eventual vocational adjustment
    4. He understands the extent to which his problems are usual and normal
    5. He has gained some appreciation of the vast amount there is to learn beyond what he now knows
  B. In his contacts with other people
    1. He has grown in awareness of the values of other people's points of view
    2. He understands the significance of individual differences in talent and interest — that individuals themselves vary from time to time and that individuals with different talents fill different functions in society
    3. He has grown in insight in regard to human growth and development and the adequacy or inadequacy of the adjustments people make
    4. He is increasingly aware of the fact that each group has its own mores and traditions, standards and values which have grown out of its particular cultural environment; hence he understands better the behavior of people in groups
  C. In his relation to the physical world and the social order in which he lives
    1. He has grown in insight into the major problems of mankind, possesses information that will aid in solving the problems of his community, understands the relation between the social and personal values of different occupations

40

2. He has a knowledge of the more basic problems facing the family and the causes that have led up to them
3. He has an accurate knowledge of the possibilities, limitations, and scope of the job area he will probably enter; knows where he can obtain specialized training and understands how to attack the problem of getting and holding a job in his own community
4. He has sufficient understanding of the great philosophies and religions to formulate a satisfying personal philosophy and a satisfying personal religion
5. He understands change as an ever-present factor in society; he knows, however, that change may be directed, that individuals have choices as to courses of action; he knows the methods that are available for changing unfavorable conditions and the effectiveness of different methods

II. Skills and techniques
   A. He is increasing his skill in personal grooming, manners, and the appearance of poise, and in body control, games, sports, and hobbies
   B. He is gaining more effective control of the communication and interpretation skills: speech, writing, reading, hearing, and general observation. He uses different speech techniques in varying situations; *i.e.*, skill in hearing enables him to follow spoken discourse, whether it is a radio talk, class lecture, informal discussion, or a sound film, as well as to follow and interpret musical compositions; so with reading, writing, and observation
   C. He is becoming more proficient in the various mental skills and techniques utilized in recognizing, analyzing, and solving problems; in generalizing; in selecting leaders and experts. He is learning to practice critical thinking in his classwork, in his personal life, in selecting and holding a job, and in his family and larger social relationships
   D. He is achieving greater mastery of the basic social skills and techniques. Drawing upon the skills and techniques listed above, he selects from them those he desires to use and can use in particular situations and thus forms a new pattern of skills or techniques. For example, the technique of putting others at their ease, so important in social adjustment, calls for manners, appearance of poise, utilization of communicative and interpretative techniques, as well as the technique of recognizing, analyzing, and solving a problem. Specific

skills and techniques included in this group are, for example, those used in meeting and introducing people, taking part in conversations (even when participants appear to have little in common to talk about), participating in discussions and social gatherings, and acting appropriately in a given social situation whether it is in the classroom, at a political gathering, a tea, or a large reception; also winning friends, leading others, or cooperating with a leader

III. Attitudes, interests, and appreciations
  A. In his thinking and judgment
    1. He is open-minded, suspending judgment though maintaining an attitude of dispassionate inquiry in which curiosity and a respect for facts and for expert opinion combine with a willingness to weigh all the evidence
    2. He has tolerance for ways of thought and behaviors different from his own, not only for those geographically and temporally remote but also for the immediate and contemporary
    3. He resists common fallacies of thought, superstitions, quick nostrums, pseudoscientific dogma, and unscrupulous propaganda
    4. He responds to his own increasing understanding of the world with a keen desire to continue his learning still further
  B. In his relations with the world outside himself
    1. He has become increasingly aware of his present and future position and responsibilities in his family and is ready to contribute his best efforts to the cooperative venture of family living
    2. He is sensitive to the contemporary scene and its implications and is motivated first to discover and then actually to make his own best contribution to society — and to make it with all the intelligence, honesty, and common sense he possesses
    3. He has deep wells of feeling that manifest themselves not only in a passionate hatred of injustice, a "divine discontent," and an unwillingness to be a passive bystander in the presence of violently pressing social issues, but also in active and joyous identification of his own happiness with the larger social good
  C. In his progress toward emotional maturity
    1. He is learning to accept the implications of his own capabilities and shortcomings, to recognize the values of

profitable and enjoyable labor, and to discover suitable avenues of release and self-expression

2. He formulates many of his own goals for thought and action and is ready to assume squarely the responsibility for his own decisions and his own actions, applying his initiative and insights to the issues that confront him and taking the full consequences for his own behavior

3. He is developing a sense of proportion, of the relevance and fitness of things, so that he can laugh at himself as well as at others and can recognize that there are some things he can do better than other people and that there are activities appropriate to people with talents different than his own

IV. Philosophy

A. He is achieving a personal philosophy which, though so dynamic and flexible that it does not tend to settle into rigid patterns and rules of thumb, also does not change so swiftly or so vacillate in direction as to lead to confusion and bewilderment

B. He is gaining a thoroughly realistic view of the world, which continually clarifies for him his relation to himself, his home and family, his fellow workers, his neighbors and fellow citizens, and his physical and social environment and helps him to see each of these as a part of an ever-changing life pattern

C. He is basing his philosophy of life firmly on personal drives toward achievable and satisfying goals, yet finding self-satisfaction incomplete without a sense of significance and usefulness to the social group. He increasingly values self and others according to work done rather than rewards gained and defines success as a balanced realization of many aims

FURTHER WORK ON COLLEGE OBJECTIVES

Simultaneously the committee began work on a more detailed statement of the original list of goals, including in it a great many examples and illustrations to add specific meaning to each one. This task is still unfinished but it should be one of the most valuable outcomes of this process of expressing the objectives of the college. The committee also tried to identify certain basic assumptions underlying these objectives, since all the goals that are set for students issue from a general point of view about the province and possibilities of general education. This outline, too, has not yet been completed, but the discussions of these assumptions have definitely helped to clarify the thinking of the committee. Indeed, the faculty of any institution might profit greatly from such an attempt to set down on paper their guiding philosophy. Illustrative of these assumptions are the following excerpts from the uncompleted statement:

1. It is important to discover the individual pattern of each student's positive capacities, needs, and interests as a basis for his education.

2. We can make progress in developing these capacities, needs, and interests within the limited time the student stays with us and within our present resources, inasmuch as all students are educable in some degree and direction.

3. Education must train for adaptability because we live in a changing society, and our offerings must be continually appraised in the light of social needs.

4. Since people do not easily generalize within and among fields of knowledge and in all basic relationships of life, we ought to help each student to generalize, to transfer, and to apply such specific knowledge.

5. It is the college's responsibility to assist each student as far as possible in making an effective adjustment to continued learning and to vocational and other out-of-college situations.

6. The purposes of general education, both within and outside the General College, may be achieved through many different media and procedures.

Another important problem on which work is still progressing is the development of objectives for each of the divisional areas. After goals for the college as a whole had been outlined, it seemed reasonable to find out what specific provisions were being made in the college program for building these desired understandings, skills, and attitudes. The coordinators of each area, in cooperation with the teaching members concerned, were therefore asked to study carefully the revised draft of General College goals and to select from this list those they considered primary instructional aims in their own area. When these had been designated by an appropriate symbol, faculty members identified the goals they considered valid teaching objectives for their courses but of considerably less importance than those placed in the first category. Finally they singled out the goals they believed might best be promoted by the educational experiences offered in other areas.

A number of instructors also prepared detailed statements of their own objectives, stating instructional outcomes more concretely than could have been done for the entire college program. Inasmuch as the appraisal study sought to determine the impact of the total program on young people rather than to appraise the contributions made by specific courses or areas, attention is not devoted to the divisional objectives in this present report. Specific objectives formulated by various members of the General College faculty for their own courses are discussed fully in other reports.[1]

[1] *Curriculum-Making in the General College*, A Report of Progress of the General College (mimeographed; Minneapolis: University of Minnesota, 1940). Ivol Spafford and others, *Building a Curriculum for General Education* (Minneapolis: University of Minnesota Press, 1943).

CHAPTER 4

Backgrounds, Interests, and Abilities of Students

Underlying every attempt to instruct or to counsel is the human equation, and no college can hope to assist a student in gaining an insight into his abilities and in selecting promising areas for his development unless his individual potentialities and motivations are known. It is not enough to know only what schools a student has previously attended, his length of stay in each one, the quality of his academic work, and his age and sex. The home from which he comes, his special aptitudes, his recreational interests, his personal adjustments and social outlook, and his hopes and goals for the future — all these, too, must be known and appreciated if the college is to serve him sympathetically and realistically. In the present study, therefore, an attempt was made to find out what types of students entered the General College and how they fared during residence there. Chapters 4 and 5 are completely devoted to a discussion of these problems, for without a clear view of the students served by this general education program and their progress in the college, it is impossible to interpret accurately the evidences gathered concerning their characteristics when they leave college.[1]

ENROLLMENT

During the eight years since the General College was established, the total enrollment of 625 students in 1932–33 has almost

[1] As indicated in Chapter 2, the present description overlaps considerably the discussion of the adolescent study, published in the current series under the title *These We Teach*. It seemed desirable, however, to find out whether the characteristics discovered by Williams and Darley in 1935–37 held for present General College students and how these traits might be related to success in the General College program. To provide the necessary data, complete records were obtained and entered on Hollerith cards for all students who entered the General College in the alternate academic years 1933–34, 1935–36, 1937–38, and 1939–40. For certain easily accessible data year-by-year studies were made.

doubled, having reached 1114 in 1939–40. This increase has been an irregular one, for attendance was highest (1234 students) in 1935–36. There was a marked decline in 1936–37, accounted for in part by a liberalizing of the entrance requirements for other colleges and in part by a general decrease in the total freshman enrollment that year. Again in 1938–39 and 1939–40 the enrollment increased, these gains coinciding with increases in almost every other division of the university. However, such fluctuations have made it rather difficult for the General College staff to forecast teaching needs from year to year.

More than three out of every four General College students now begin their work in the fall quarter, the rest entering in the winter and spring quarters. The number of students who transfer into the college from other branches of the university during the year does not entirely offset the number who drop out after one or two quarters, so that attendance in any single quarter is usually less than three fourths of the total yearly enrollment.

Men have always outnumbered women in the General College by a three to two ratio, which differs little from the ratio prevailing in the arts college and in the university as a whole. The fact that more men than women attend the General College does, however, have definite implications for curriculum planning and vocational counseling.

HOME BACKGROUND

Almost three fourths of all General College students come from homes in the Twin City area, a proportion somewhat higher than in other colleges of the university.[2] In the arts college, for example, about three fifths of the students come from the Minneapolis and St. Paul area, and only slightly more than half of the total university enrollment is drawn from the immediate locality. The number of General College students coming from out-of-state high schools has declined (only 3 per cent recently as compared with 10 per cent in the earlier years), although for

[2] To conserve space, tables have been omitted for all data that are not rather directly related to appraisal of the General College program. The complete tables, presenting a year-by-year analysis of the data, are on file in the offices of the University Committee on Educational Research, University of Minnesota.

47

the university at large the proportion of students drawn from other states and foreign countries has increased. Students of lesser academic ability who live near the university apparently often experiment with a quarter or a year of college training, whereas young people of the same degree of scholastic aptitude who live at a distance are not as likely to take a college course. The fact that so many General College students live in the immediate vicinity of the university also suggests that their campus contacts may be limited largely to those made in the classroom. Attending the university thus extends but does not radically alter the home and school environment to which they have been so long accustomed.

As may be expected from the foregoing facts, most General College students live with their parents while they attend the university. The minority live in dormitories, rooming houses, or in the homes of relatives or friends. Less than 2 per cent of the total group live in fraternity or sorority houses or have apartments of their own.

Most of these young people are the children of native-born parents. The fathers of about a fourth of the men and a fifth of the women came from some foreign country, predominantly Scandinavian; a smaller percentage of the mothers were born elsewhere. English is spoken exclusively in about three fourths of the homes represented and is employed most of the time in the others. Hence the linguistic difficulties that often arise when another language is used extensively in the home do not to any great degree explain the low verbal aptitude scores made by these students.

About a third of both the fathers and the mothers attended only an elementary school; the rest had taken at least some high school work. Less than a sixth of the fathers and less than a tenth of the mothers had received college degrees, and about a sixth of these parents had elected special cultural or vocational courses in addition to their regular academic work. On the whole, therefore, although General College students do not come from homes with strong college traditions, their parents have had more formal education than people at large.

Reasonably normal family relationships seem to prevail in the students' homes, for more than three fourths of these young people stated that their parents were living together. In only 3 per cent of the cases were the parents separated or divorced, in another 6 per cent remarriage had occurred, but whether it was preceded by death or divorce was not indicated. Almost 10 per cent of the students came from homes broken by the death of one or both parents. One student in eight was an only child; the majority came from families having two, three, or four children. Oldest, middle, and youngest children were equally represented, suggesting that in a state university, where tuition is low, all children in a family may have about equal chances of attending college.

ECONOMIC AND CULTURAL BACKGROUND

The occupations of the fathers afford some clues to the general economic level of the homes from which these young people come. When types of jobs reported were classified according to the Minnesota Occupational Scale, the results showed conclusively that middle-class homes furnished the bulk of General College students. About one student in three had a father employed in professional, semiprofessional, or managerial work; the fathers of the others were largely proprietors of small businesses, salesmen, office clerks, and semiskilled workmen. Although only 1 per cent of the students came from the homes of common laborers, a great many students could undoubtedly not have attended a college with higher tuition fees. When the socio-economic rating of the home was related to the length of time the student remained in the General College, it appeared that those from financially circumscribed homes were at no disadvantage. To many of these young people of limited economic resources a state university, with its low tuition fees, had opened a door of opportunity that must otherwise have remained closed.

The amount of financial support that students expected to obtain from their parents while they attended the university corroborates this general picture of middle-class status. At entrance to college more than half the men and a fourth of the women hoped

49

to support themselves totally or partially. The number of men who actually held some type of part-time job included, by the end of the year, two thirds of the whole freshman class. In many individual cases this work load was far too heavy to accompany a full academic program. For example, one out of every four men holding an outside job worked upwards of thirty-seven hours a week, and every fourth woman who held a part-time job worked twenty-eight hours or more a week.

Before entering college almost half the students had traveled some distance from Minnesota, visiting the seacoasts or traveling extensively elsewhere in the United States. Yet more than a fourth of all entering freshmen reported no traveling, and another fourth visited only the nearby states. Upon any program of general education must rest a special obligation to guard such young people against provincialism in their social outlook.

A majority of these young people (55 per cent) came from Protestant homes. One student in five attended a Catholic church; one in eight was Jewish; the remainder stated no religious preference.

The types of magazines read at entrance to college also helped to suggest the general cultural level of the homes represented. Three magazines, on the average, were reported as being read regularly, though women students listed more titles than men students did. Most popular among those mentioned by both sexes were the *Reader's Digest, Life, Time, Saturday Evening Post,* and *Collier's,* in the order mentioned. For women students the *Ladies' Home Journal, Good Housekeeping,* and *McCall's* also ranked near the top. *Harpers* was read by less than 3 per cent of the total entering class, the *New Republic* by one student in 500.

HIGH SCHOOL BACKGROUND

The typical General College student in 1939–40 was a member of a high school graduating class of 330 students, which was more than twice as large as the high school graduating class from which the typical student had come eight years earlier. A fifth of those who entered in 1939–40 graduated in classes of 500 students, and another fifth in classes of less than 100 members. During this eight-year period there was a decrease in the number of those from out-of-state secondary schools. Students coming from very small high schools must have encountered particularly difficult problems in adapting themselves to the academic and social life of a large university.

The average General College student is not a typical high school graduate in his scholastic achievement, as Figure 1 shows,

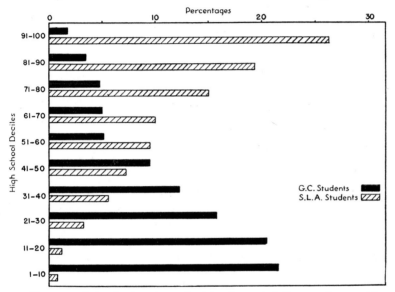

Figure 1. High school ranks attained by General College students and by students in the College of Science, Literature, and the Arts (S.L.A.).

since he is surpassed in this respect by two thirds of those who receive high school diplomas. Less than a tenth of all General College entrants had graduated in the upper quarter of their high school classes. Many of these students had found themselves ineligible for admission to the college of their first choice because they did not present the required number of units of work in certain special fields. Each year, of course, a few superior students enter the college because they definitely want to obtain a general education before they enter special fields of study.

Since this college was established especially to meet the needs of young people who were not faring well in the traditional arts college curriculum, impressive differences are to be expected in the measured academic abilities of General College students and those entering other colleges of the university. The below-average high school rating of General College students contrasts sharply, for example, with the situation in the College of Science, Literature, and the Arts, where the typical student now attains a high school percentile rank of 79, superior to three fourths of all high school graduates.[3] The fact that this rank is significantly higher than the average high school rating (65) of the arts college students in the years immediately preceding the opening of the General College shows that the establishment of the new unit has resulted in more homogeneous populations in both colleges. Certainly these statistics reveal clearly that instructors in the General College face a strikingly different teaching problem than do faculty members in other colleges, and one for which new curriculum materials and new techniques are required.

More than half of all General College students enter the university with only twelve academic secondary school units, the minimum required for high school graduation. Since less than 10 per cent begin their college work with thirteen units or more, we may infer that most students have taken few elective courses in high school. For this reason a broad program of general education in college may be more important for these young people than for the academically more able students who may have browsed widely during their secondary school years.

The academic interests of General College students were suggested by the kinds of high school subjects they especially liked or disliked and those they singled out as most difficult and easiest for them. Both men and women students definitely preferred the social studies; such nonacademic subjects as art, music, home economics, and shop surprisingly enough ranked second; sciences

[3] The high school rating of Science, Literature, and the Arts students, which is very similar to that attained by Institute of Technology and School of Nursing students, is considerably higher than that of students in several other colleges of the university. The average score attained by students in these other divisions, however, surpasses decisively the General College averages, ranking some twenty percentile points higher. This still allows, of course, for a great deal of overlapping in the abilities of students enrolled in the various colleges.

ranked third for men, and English for women. Distinct sex differences emerged at this point: English and foreign languages were definitely preferred by the women students and mathematics by the men. This general pattern of subject interests differs significantly from preferences expressed by superior students, who usually evince far keener enthusiasm for foreign languages and mathematics and relatively less enthusiasm for the social studies and nonacademic subjects.

When students singled out their most and least difficult high school subjects, the courses they considered easiest were usually those they liked best, and vice versa. Social studies and nonacademic courses were judged the easiest; mathematics, by a decisive vote, was considered the most difficult. Again, pronounced differences appeared between the sexes; men found English a much more difficult subject than women did, and women felt the same way about the social sciences.

The proportion of students who enter the General College after taking some university work elsewhere has declined in recent years, from 38 per cent in 1933 to 19 per cent in 1939–40, as Figure 2 indicates. This fact definitely suggests that the university is now making a more appropriate initial distribution of its students. Since the College of Science, Literature, and the Arts contributes more young people to the General College than all other divisions, most of the transferred students have had a smattering of liberal arts courses. The College of Education, the College of Agriculture, Forestry, and Home Economics, and the Institute of Technology supply most of the remaining transfer students. Less than 5 per cent of all General College entrants have taken college work at institutions other than the University of Minnesota.

Figure 3 reveals that between 1933 and 1940 most students who came directly from high school were referred to the General College because of inadequate high school marks or low test performance. Those who had had previous college training usually came because they had been dropped or placed on probation

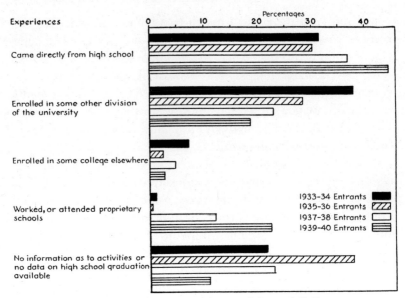

Experiences | Percentages

Came directly from high school

Enrolled in some other division of the university

Enrolled in some college elsewhere

Worked, or attended proprietary schools

No information as to activities or no data on high school graduation available

1933-34 Entrants
1935-36 Entrants
1937-38 Entrants
1939-40 Entrants

Figure 2. Previous educational experiences of General College entrants.

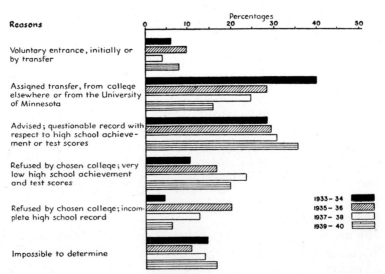

Reasons | Percentages

Voluntary entrance, initially or by transfer

Assigned transfer, from college elsewhere or from the University of Minnesota

Advised; questionable record with respect to high school achievement or test scores

Refused by chosen college; very low high school achievement and test scores

Refused by chosen college; incomplete high school record

Impossible to determine

1933-34
1935-36
1937-38
1939-40

Figure 3. Reasons for entering the General College, as indicated by scholastic records.

54

in the college of their initial enrollment. Less than 10 per cent of all students entered the General College with academic records that would have entitled them to enroll without restriction or probationary status in another college.

Young people who began their college work elsewhere had spent from one to nine or more quarters in residence there, with an average length of stay of two quarters. These young people had for the most part barely commenced their programs in these units before inappropriate choice of courses, changes in vocational goals, or seeming incompetence resulted in their transfer to the General College. Only an occasional student was transferred with an acceptable record; the rest had either been dropped, placed on probation, or given grades so low that some change in their educational program appeared highly advisable. Most students who enter the General College, therefore, must attain not only some measure of general education but also a fundamental academic and vocational reorientation.

One student out of every five had delayed his entrance to the General College for some time after graduating from high school, but no data existed to show what he had been doing in this period. These intervening activities, as well as the slow progress many of these young people made in elementary and secondary school, account for the fact that General College students are about a year older at entrance than are freshmen in other colleges.

ABILITIES AND APTITUDES

Although General College students resemble closely the whole range of young people of their own age group in their ability to deal with abstract verbal symbols, they are definitely at some disadvantage when compared with other university students and with high school graduates in general. On the American Council Psychological Examination, as shown in Figure 4, the typical entrant to the General College ranks at about the thirty-seventh percentile of the high school senior distribution and at about the tenth percentile of that of freshmen in the College of Science, Literature, and the Arts. Whereas the range of scores is almost as im-

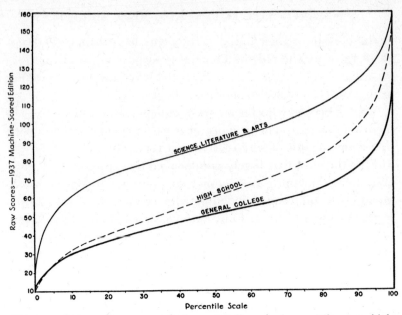

Figure 4. Comparative scores of General College freshmen, Minnesota high school graduates, and freshmen in the College of Science, Literature, and the Arts on the American Council Psychological Examination.

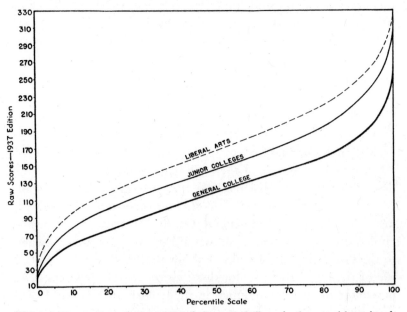

Figure 5. Comparison of the scores of General College freshmen with national norms for the American Council Psychological Examination.

pressive in the General College as in the arts college, indicating that counselors and teachers in both colleges must provide for occasional students of extremely high or low ability, the levels to which classroom teaching must be geared are notably different.

The score made by the typical General College freshman ranks him at approximately the twenty-second percentile for liberal arts colleges elsewhere and slightly higher, at the thirty-fifth percentile, for junior colleges throughout the country, as may be seen in Figure 5. Such differences must be interpreted with caution, for variations in the aims of colleges should definitely lead to differences in the kinds of students selected. A college that conceives its mission to be the training of the scholarly few ought to be thoroughly alarmed if its rating is not well above that of the typical liberal arts college. But if the college is honestly trying to meet the needs of most young people in the community a ranking as high as the national arts college median should be equally disquieting. Comparisons with other colleges simply serve to describe the General College in its broader social setting, so that differences may be understood and taken into account in evaluating the education given these young people.

On the Miller Analogies Test (Form B), a penetrating measure of verbal aptitude widely used at the University of Minnesota, the average score made by General College entrants is the equivalent of a forty-fourth percentile for sophomores in the College of Education and a first percentile for sophomores in the College of Science, Literature, and the Arts, or, expressed in terms of its IQ equivalent, an IQ of about 106. Darley and Williams reached an almost identical estimate (an average IQ of 107) after comparing American Council Psychological Examination scores and their IQ equivalents. For the lowest fourth, estimates of IQ's cannot be made, since the scores fall outside Miller's tabled values. For the highest fourth, who attained raw scores of 50 or greater, the equivalent IQ would be approximately 111 or higher.

The Cooperative English Test, a broad measure of usage, spelling, and vocabulary, which is administered to Minnesota high school seniors each spring, provides further descriptive data concerning General College students.[4] Again it appears that seniors who subsequently enter the General College are as a group at some disadvantage in comparison with their high school colleagues and possess distinctly less linguistic skill, as measured by this test, than other freshmen on the Minnesota campus. The score made by the typical General College student, for example, earns him a twentieth percentile rating on all-university norms for this test, indicating about the same degree of handicap as was evidenced on general aptitude tests. Men students possessed these linguistic skills to a lesser degree than women — a finding corroborated by many studies. Results from these verbal tests, therefore, clearly suggest that for these students symbolical presentations alone may not be sufficient to build desired meanings and that more concrete and more specific learning materials may be needed to arouse interest and develop adequate understandings.

The Wesley Test of Social Terms, designed to measure students' acquaintance with basic social, political, and economic concepts, was also given to General College entrants in 1938 and 1939. From the rather limited normative data available it would appear that General College students are reasonably typical of high school seniors in their understanding of social terms. About a fourth of the General College entrants showed the same level of comprehension as eleventh-grade students; another fourth approximated the performance of college freshmen. The fact that as a rule women students did not do well on this test corroborated their tendency to rank social studies as rather difficult for them.

Like other academic groups General College students made higher scores on the Minnesota Clerical Workers' Test than unselected adults. On both the numbers and the names sections the average rating for men students corresponded to approximately the seventy-fifth percentile in the general population distribution, and women ranked even higher. When compared with estab-

[4] Instead of tables or charts to show the initial status of General College students, general statements only are given here. In later chapters, where outcomes are investigated, both the initial and final status of General College young people will be presented to show the extent of gains made on various tests.

lished clerical workers, however, they were at some disadvantage. The typical General College girl was surpassed by approximately three out of every four employed clerical workers, and men students showed even less aptitude for clerical tasks.

ATTITUDES AND ADJUSTMENTS

On the Minnesota Personality Scale, a new test of personal and social adjustment, no outside normative data are yet available.[5] The characteristics that seem to be indicated by high scores on each of the subtests are set forth below.

I. Good morale; a cheerful, optimistic outlook
II. Good social adjustments; liking for people and skill in social relationships
III. Good family adjustments
IV. Good emotional and health adjustments
V. Conservatism in economic outlook

General College entrants are quite similar to freshmen in the College of Science, Literature, and the Arts in the traits measured by this inventory, a particularly interesting finding in view of the notable differences discovered on many other tests. In the ten comparisons made (five for men and five for women, since different tests are used for the two sexes) only two differences between arts college and General College students met the 1 per cent criterion of significance. These revealed a tendency for arts college women to be more liberal in their social attitudes and more cheerful or generally optimistic in their outlook. The one difference that satisfied the 5 per cent level of significance indicated that arts college men were also less conservative in their economic beliefs than their General College colleagues. On the whole, General College performance on this test corroborates the results from the Bell Personality Inventory, which likewise indicated that in their social adjustments General College students ranked almost the same as did academically superior groups.

Interesting light on how General College students view themselves is afforded by their responses to characteristics listed on a

[5] J. G. Darley and W. J. McNamara, *Minnesota Personality Scale* (New York: Psychological Corporation, 1941).

59

basic information sheet filled out when they entered college. Each student checked as many adjectives in a given list as he considered actually descriptive of himself. The most frequently endorsed adjective was *friendly*, singled out by four fifths of the men and women. Next in importance were *cheerful*, checked by half the students, and *conscientious*, *patient*, and *calm*, designated by at least one student in every three. Few students considered themselves talented or persevering, nor did more than an occasional student exhibit neurotic tendencies. These self-evaluations tend to substantiate the pattern of personality characteristics gained from tests and observational data. On the whole General College students appear to be friendly, likable young people, capable of adjusting themselves to other people with ease and graciousness but not distinguished by special scholastic talent or the drive necessary to realize fully their potentialities.

The attitudes of General College students on social, political, and economic questions were explored in the Pace situations test. On this test of liberalism and conservatism the typical attitudes of men and women entrants were found to be almost identical with those discovered for other undergraduate groups. As was true for these other populations, the distribution of attitudes indicated the presence of more extremely conservative than extremely liberal students.

At entrance to college, students appeared to be keenly interested in such recreational activities as listening to the radio (predominantly to variety, popular music, and sports programs and to news commentators), reading newspapers and popular news magazines and digests, and going to the movies. Other activities frequently engaged in by General College entrants were team competitions of an athletic type, field sports (such as hunting, fishing, hiking, and riding), dancing, and conversing freely with acquaintances and strangers. Most students belonged to two or three clubs, chiefly of a social type, but only a small minority engaged in any artistic or musical activities, did free writing of any sort, held positions of leadership in school or extracurricular activities, did carpentry or experimentation in chemistry or physics, or had hobbies that claimed much time.

BACKGROUNDS, INTERESTS, AND ABILITIES

EDUCATIONAL AND VOCATIONAL PLANS

What General College students anticipate in the way of further education and eventual employment also reveals a good deal concerning the hopes and plans of young people served by this general education program. Among factors that influenced their attendance at some college or university, General College freshmen ranked first the statement "I realize a need for a broad education to prepare me for life outside the job." Closely following this were these reasons, in the order mentioned: "To get specific training for the job of my choice," "I didn't know what I wanted to do and thought college would help me decide," "I wanted help and guidance leading to a wise vocational choice," and "College is necessary to achieve a business and social position." Women students were somewhat less concerned than men about specific job training, though they too wished to check the validity of their vocational choices. The social values of college attendance and the friends young people may make by coming to the university held a somewhat stronger appeal for women than for men students. General College students were inclined to regard college as a means of exploring their abilities, whereas students in the College of Science, Literature, and the Arts were somewhat more concerned about the values of specific job and preprofessional training.

In indicating reasons why they had selected the University of Minnesota for higher education General College students — both men and women and those of higher and lower academic ability — attached first importance to the nearness of the university to their homes. Next in significance was the fact that the university has high educational standards. For women the next three reasons were that Minnesota is a large, well-known university, that their friends attended that university, and that tuition and living costs were low. Men gave the same reasons but shifted the order, emphasizing the financial factor as the third most important reason and dropping the influence of friends to fifth place. Arts college students gave exactly the same reasons for selecting the University of Minnesota that these General College freshmen did.

61

OUTCOMES OF GENERAL EDUCATION

Over 40 per cent of those who entered the General College in the fall of 1938–39 had hoped to be admitted to the College of Science, Literature, and the Arts. This proportion would have been considerably higher if figures on students who transferred into the General College at the beginning of the winter and spring quarters were included in these data. The College of Education, the Institute of Technology, and the College of Agriculture, Forestry, and Home Economics were the most popular of the remaining choices. About a seventh of the freshman entrants indicated that they intended initially to come to the General College; another fourth gave no indication at all of what division of the university they had planned originally to enter.

When these young people entered the General College they thought they would be staying approximately three quarters. Completion of the program, evidenced by receipt of the Associate in Arts degree, was expected by only two fifths of the women and one fourth of the men; another fourth outlined no further school plans. One student in five stated flatly that he had no intention of obtaining a college degree. A majority of those who did not plan to take the A.A. degree indicated that they were looking forward to degrees from other colleges — predominantly arts, education, and engineering — or to certificates in nursing. The extent to which these ambitious plans were changed during General College residence constitutes a searching test of the reorientation provided by this experimental college. Evidence on this point is presented in Chapter 6.

A similar lack of realism was evident in the vocational plans of General College students. Again and again young people of limited academic ability and financial resources looked forward to careers involving extended professional training. Though less than a third of the fathers of General College students held positions classified in the two top brackets of the Minnesota Occupational Scale, about half the choices given by students who had decided upon a vocation involved these professional and managerial posts. This is some measure of improvement over the situation discovered by Williams and Darley in 1935, when almost two thirds of all General College students aspired to top-ranking

62

jobs. The most frequently stated vocational goals for men were "business" (with the particular field unspecified), engineering, teaching, accounting, embalming, and law, in the order mentioned; and for women the top-ranking goals were nursing, teaching, business, designing, and social work.

Coupled with many of these inappropriate and often highly mistaken choices was a disturbing attitude of certainty or fixity in choice. Students who considered their choices as absolutely fixed or reasonably certain (almost half the entire group) outnumbered by more than a two to one ratio those who stated that they were somewhat doubtful or extremely uncertain as to the appropriateness of their present vocational goals. Only one student in five, for example, was ready to admit that he had doubts as to the wisdom of his present choice.

Still more disquieting was the outlook of these young people on the problem of job training. Almost two out of every three students expected that the university and the university alone would make them ready for their life work. Of the remainder, men placed greater confidence than women in apprenticeship on the job, whereas more women staked their hopes on attendance at a private vocational school. The fact that these young people were relying chiefly on the university for their job training means that those who drop out of school without completing their courses not only fail to carry through educational plans but are also forced to change drastically, and usually blindly, their vocational objectives.

Why these young people made the choices they did, however unrealistic they might be, is suggested by the factors to which they attributed their vocational decisions. From a list of nine possible reasons given in the basic information sheet, each student singled out as many as he felt had definitely influenced his own choice. A few students listed others in the spaces provided for such additions. The outstanding reason for both men and women was liking for the work, specified by more than two thirds. Second in importance was the belief that they knew a lot about it, mentioned by a quarter of the students. Men and women differed rather significantly in the importance they attached to the remaining reasons. Men seemed more influenced by the fact that their fathers and close relatives worked in the field, that the financial outlook was promising, and that the choice was a good one in the light of the present economic situation. Women attached slightly more importance to the urgings of parents and relatives and to the possibility that the job offered "the best way to use my abilities."

SUMMARY

These, then, are the General College students — young people typical, in their abilities, their interests, their social attitudes, and their hopes and plans for the future, of the great masses of American high school graduates. If these young people had completed high school two decades or so ago, the vast majority of them would have found jobs and joined immediately the ranks of undistinguished middle-class men and women. But today many seek a year, two years, or often four years of college training. The fact that these young people have not shown thorough competence for the usual secondary school curriculum does not mean that they might not profit from suitable courses at the university. If anything, it would appear that they are less ready to stand on their own feet and hence need definite, systematic preparation for their out-of-school responsibilities.

Most of these young people possess neither the types of abstract intelligence, the special scholastic aptitudes, nor the patterning of interests to permit them to embark successfully on the usual liberal arts program. Instead they require very specific and clear orientation to their oncoming adult responsibilities — a clarification of problems of personal adjustment, the formulation of a reasonable vocational choice and of realistic plans for obtaining and holding a job, a preparation for home and family responsibilities, and a broadened understanding and appreciation of sociocivic relationships in their own communities, in the state, and in the nation.

CHAPTER 5

Progress in the General College

The General College attempts to provide appropriate educational experiences for young people whose needs cannot be met by the four-year liberal arts college. In order to evaluate properly this program of general education we must know the length of time these students remain in college and the kinds of learning opportunities of which they avail themselves while there. It is evident, of course, as the Pennsylvania studies[1] and hosts of others definitely show, that neither a student's length of stay nor his exposure to certain courses can insure the attainment of desirable educational outcomes. But it is also true that the college cannot really help a student to develop fundamental concepts, to broaden his acquaintance with contemporary problems, and to reach realistic decisions about his educational and vocational future unless he stays in college long enough to receive such assistance. For these reasons a careful study was made of students' length of residence in the college, the kinds of courses they elected, and the general characteristics of those who completed the two-year program and received the Associate in Arts degree.

LENGTH OF RESIDENCE

Although the General College offers two complete years of general education, only a small proportion of its students have availed themselves of the full program. Just about a fourth of all entering students complete five or more quarters of General College work.[2] Some students are transferred to other divisions

[1] W. W. Learned and B. W. Wood, *The Student and His Knowledge* (New York: Carnegie Foundation for the Advancement of Teaching, 1938).

[2] Five quarters, instead of six, are considered to be the equivalent of the full program because many students transfer into the General College at the beginning of the winter quarter from other divisions and are therefore eligible to complete their course in five quarters.

during these first two years, but of all General College students, those who remain in the college and those who transfer, only one in every four elects more than six quarters of work at the university. The average length of time that students remain in the General College is slightly less than three full quarters, as may be seen in Figure 6. In other words, whatever measure of general education can be achieved through courses designed to this end must be gained by the typical General College student in a single academic year. In terms of university credits we may say that he has but forty quarter hours in which to become "at home" in

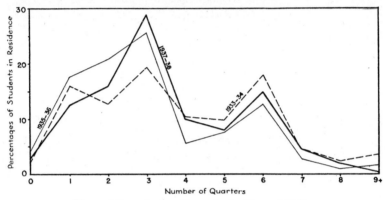

Figure 6. Length of residence in the General College.

all the worlds — biological, physical, social, literary, artistic, and psychological — to which the General College seeks to orient him. This necessarily implies that all teaching efforts must be sharply focused on important goals.

Students who enter the college in the fall quarter have the best prospect of remaining in school. Of those who enter in the spring quarter, most of them transfers from other colleges, almost half of the men and a third of the women remain only for that quarter. In view of the brief stay of winter- and spring-quarter entrants, then, short-term courses appear particularly appropriate. However, whether they enter in the fall, winter, or spring quarters, the intervention of the summer vacation brings about the largest loss of students to the college.

Another method of determining how long students stay in the

66

General College is to compare the numbers who leave at the end of each quarter. During the last eight years there has been some slight improvement in persistence, illustrated by the fact that 70 per cent of those who entered in the fall quarter in 1933 remained in the General College throughout the year, in comparison with 76 per cent of those who entered in the fall of 1939. The problem still remains a serious one, however, as may be seen in Table 1. Fifteen per cent of the students enrolled in the General College during the fall quarter do not return for the winter quarter; 15 per cent of the winter-quarter enrollees do not return for the spring quarter. Over 50 per cent of those who have entered at any time during one year do not return the next year. In individual courses there is an even greater turnover.

TABLE 1. PERSISTENCE IN GENERAL COLLEGE ATTENDANCE

Percentages of Students	1933–34	1935–36	1937–38	1939–40
Enrolled at some time in the year; did not return winter quarter	15.5	17.5	14.1	13.2
Enrolled in winter quarter; did not return spring quarter	17.6	18.8	15.4	12.1
Enrolled in spring quarter; did not return the next fall quarter	32.3	52.8	51.2	44.6
Enrolled at some time in the year; returned the following year	51.4	34.4	37.7	44.8

The relatively small percentage of young people who enroll for a second year indicates one important instructional problem faced by the General College faculty. Since only two out of every five young people return the following fall, second-year students are in a distinct minority, constituting less than a third of the student body in a given year. Inasmuch as General College courses seldom have prerequisites, new and old students are usually found in the same classes, carrying on much the same activities.

The length of time that a young person remains in the General College does not seem to be dependent on his measured aptitude for academic tasks. Those whom college aptitude tests identify as clearly able to profit from the usual type of college work (students with scores above the average for the combined arts college and General College populations) or as poor academic risks (students with aptitude ratings that fall below the fifteenth percentile on university norms) remain in the General College about the same number of quarters. Students who drop out without completing the program seldom leave because they are forced to, by course failures. In the selection that occurs during the freshman and sophomore years in institutions with strongly academic goals, verbal intelligence is the most important factor. The fact that the General College tends to retain students irrespective of their academic ability may be interpreted in different ways, depending on one's philosophy of post-secondary education. If the General College is conceived of primarily as a feeder to liberal arts colleges, which it was not intended to be, more rigorous selection would be eminently desirable. But if the college is designed to serve young people of merely average academic ability, then teachers are perhaps to be commended for not failing a great many students simply because they do not measure up to stereotyped conceptions of what college students should know and do.

Within this common period of residence, however, students of high academic ability much more frequently take so-called combination programs, involving courses in other divisions of the university (36 per cent of the students of higher academic ability as compared with 20 per cent of those of lower academic ability). They more often receive A.A. degrees or transfer to other colleges. About 18 per cent of all students who enter the General College with college aptitude ratings of fifty or above receive A. A. degrees, in contrast to 7 per cent of those enrolling with ratings of fifteen or below. Students in this higher aptitude group likewise have double the chance of transferring successfully to another college of the university.

THE KINDS OF COURSES GENERAL COLLEGE STUDENTS TAKE

Four broad orientation areas, established in 1938, provide for the study and discussion of problems relating to individual adjustment, home and family relations, vocational orientation, and socio-civic affairs. In addition, the General College offers courses in seven subject-matter areas — psychology; physical science; human development; euthenics; literature, speech, and writing; general arts; and social science.[3] From these eleven areas the student chooses three each year as a basis for planning his program and completing the requirement that he pass three comprehensive examinations annually, or six in the two years, to receive his A.A. degree. He usually takes two or three courses (twelve to eighteen credit hours) in each area he selects. By these means the General College attempts to acquaint its students with major problems in many fields of contemporary living.

How long a young person attends college is undoubtedly far less important than what he does while he is there — the character of the courses he takes, the general pattern of his academic program, and the quality of his achievement. During his General College residence the typical student takes work in five divisional areas, although in some of them he may elect only one single-quarter course. About 15 per cent of these young people have had contacts with only one, two, or three of the eleven major areas; another 15 per cent have taken courses that suggest at least a rudimentary acquaintance with eight, nine, ten, or even eleven areas. This wide variance certainly suggests striking differences in the degree of general education obtained by the groups of students involved.

Because these students are not bound by any specific course requirements, the particular areas in which they tend to elect their work are also of interest. In these eight years about two thirds of all students have registered for courses in the areas of psychology, current affairs, or literature, speech, and writing. Almost half have elected courses classified in the economics, biology, and history and government areas; a third, or fewer, have sampled courses in the areas of social problems, physical science, general arts, or euthenics.[4] During the two years (1938–

[3] These areas have changed slightly from year to year; the present listings correspond to the titles of the areas in 1939–40.

[4] The areas listed here include several in which comprehensive examinations were offered only during the earlier years of the program. When the orientation areas were introduced certain subject-matter areas were consolidated, yielding the seven listed above.

40) in which the four orientation areas have been offered, the typical student elected two of these areas his first year and usually added a third if he returned for a second year. A few courses have been elected by approximately half of all General College enrollees — for example, Current Affairs, Practical Applications of Psychology, Writing Laboratory, Formation of Public Opinion, Human Biology, Literature Today, and Our Economic Life. In the early years of the program there was an especially heavy loading of social studies courses, many of which were dropped and the materials incorporated in the new orientation courses. Courses in which more than 40 per cent of all freshman students were enrolled in 1939–40 were Socio-Civic Orientation, Individual Orientation, Practical Applications of Psychology, Writing Laboratory, and Vocational Orientation. Many of these popular courses are quite obviously selected because they contribute toward several of the comprehensive areas rather than because of their intrinsic interest or their reputation. Business Mathematics, for example, is credited only in the vocational area, whereas Psychology could be credited in any one of four areas.

Whether students tend to remain in a given course throughout the year or whether they drift in or out of it at the end of the fall or winter quarters also makes a difference in the teaching of a course. In a study limited to students in residence throughout the year 1939–40 the percentage of those enrolled in full-year courses who actually took all three quarters of work exceeded 50 for only five of the sixteen such courses offered that year. On the average only a third of the students who remain in school for the entire year take all three quarters of the courses in which they happen to be enrolled. If all the students enrolled in a course were considered, instead of only those who remained in school throughout the entire year, the proportion of persisting students would be still more sharply reduced. A General College instructor must thus constantly remember the widely varying backgrounds of his students, even with respect to the materials he has covered earlier in the same year.

Students outside the General College also elect certain courses given in the college, notably those in human biology and physical science, to meet their own degree requirements. In 1937–38 there were eighteen one-quarter courses in which at least a tenth of the students came from other colleges; in 1939–40 the number of such courses had declined to seven. In both years, however, General College and non-General College students achieved at strikingly different levels. In 1939–40, for example, in the three courses that drew more than a third of their students from outside the General College, the median percentiles for General College and non-General College students on the final achievement tests were 39 and 70, 38 and 73, and 44 and 66.

When the General College students enrolled in various courses were compared on a number of measures, the most impressive finding was the absence of differences. True, the student's sex affects his choice of courses to some extent. Euthenics attracted 62 per cent of the women and about 20 per cent of the men, and general arts courses were also more frequently elected by women. Men were more likely to take courses in economics (80 per cent versus 40 per cent of the women) and physical science (43 per cent versus 16 per cent of the women). Yet no other difference met even a 5 per cent criterion of significance.[5] The enrollment in almost every course yielded a cross section of the entire General College student body with respect to aptitude and previous academic achievement. The present lack of differences among courses contrasts sharply with the situation in most secondary schools and colleges, where a certain hierarchy of offerings can almost always be discovered — the more academically able students being attracted to certain courses and those less able drawn to others. Whatever the explanation for this lack of distinction among General College classes may be, it has important educational implications, since it means that each in-

[5] Tests of statistical significance have been applied throughout this study to all observed differences. Whenever a difference is characterized as significant it meets the 1 per cent criterion of significance, showing that such a difference could have arisen less than one time in a hundred as a result of errors of random sampling. A few differences that are significant only at the 5 per cent level (five chances in a hundred that the difference represents a sampling error) are pointed out, but the inconclusive nature of this difference is always indicated.

71

structor in his own classroom must provide for almost the whole range of individual differences found within the college.

ACHIEVEMENT IN COMPREHENSIVE EXAMINATIONS

Students who make normal progress in the college complete three comprehensive examinations each year, presumably after about fifteen quarter hours' preparation for each one. Yet an analysis of the records compiled during these eight years discloses that a third of all students have not passed comprehensive examinations, as may be seen in Figure 7. In 1939–40, 36 per

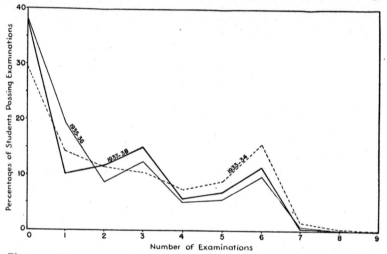

Figure 7. The number of comprehensive examinations passed by students during their residence in the General College.

cent of the freshmen who had remained in college throughout the year took no comprehensives at the end of the spring quarter, a proportion very similar to the 33 per cent found for 1933–34, the earliest year studied. More than a third of the freshmen, in other words, make little effort to meet the college requirement that they pass three comprehensive examinations during each year of residence. Nevertheless the encouraging increase in the numbers who have taken three examinations at the conclusion of the first year's work (25 per cent in 1933–34 to 40 per cent in 1939–40) shows that more young people are now making some effort to fulfill this requirement. For students who attempt one

72

or more examinations, the median number passed during their entire period of General College residence has been slightly less than three (Figure 7).

Students who try the comprehensive examinations have had considerably more extensive training in the field involved than have the general run of students. Those taking examinations in 1933–35 averaged approximately nine quarter hours' credit in each area tested, whereas students in 1937–39 offered almost twelve quarter hours. At least one fourth of all those students who tried the comprehensive examinations had actually had less work than the general run of students in the fields covered; conversely, many young people who never applied for an examination in a certain area had had sufficient course work to enable them to pass that examination successfully. If the fact that many young people pass the comprehensive examinations without fulfilling the expected fifteen hours of preparatory work means that mastery of a field has been valued above the amassing of a stereotyped number of credits, it represents a desirable condition. It is highly undesirable, however, if it indicates that students have been passed irrespective of the quality of their examination performance.

Furthermore the amount of preparation for these comprehensive examinations varies significantly with the areas concerned. For examinations in such fields as economics, physical science, and literature, speech, and writing, the average student has each year presented almost fifteen quarter hours of preparatory work. For other examinations barely half this amount of preparation has been offered. Illustrative are the current affairs area, in which six and a half hours was the average over the entire period, and biology and euthenics, in which the average was seldom as high as nine hours. In no instance did the typical student present more than the specified fifteen hours. In view of this situation the college's requirements for graduation could be met with considerably less than two full years' work.

The wide diversity in the combinations of comprehensives that students took in any one year was revealed in a careful study of the programs of all those who tried any comprehensive examinations in 1939–40. For only four combinations of areas were there more than fifteen students taking the same pattern of comprehensives. Thus in that year 32 students took examinations in socio-civic orientation and vocational orientation and tried no third comprehensive examination; 22 students took examinations in vocational orientation, socio-civic orientation, and literature, speech, and writing; 17 students took examinations in socio-civic orientation, individual orientation, and literature, speech, and writing; another 17 took examinations in socio-civic orientation, vocational orientation, and physical science. Except in the case of the social science comprehensive, for which the socio-civic orientation comprehensive has been a prerequisite, and the euthenics comprehensive, which presupposes successful completion of the home life orientation comprehensive examination, there was little evidence that a given examination was more often elected by freshmen than by sophomores, or vice versa.

General College comprehensive examinations have always been graded on a relative basis; that is, certain stated proportions of the students have been assigned A's, B's, C's, and D's and the lowest 10 per cent have been failed, although some instructors have set other thresholds for the F grade. Because there is no established threshold or level of scores that students must attain if they are to pass a test, direct studies could not be made of the special abilities required for successful performance in these tests. Nor was it possible to determine the type of preparation needed to reach a stated level of mastery in a given field. It is therefore impossible to determine whether standards have been gradually raised or relaxed during these eight years or whether the present passing levels are really appropriate for the students concerned. Studies of the scores made by students on these comprehensive examinations reveal in a general way, however, what types of young people tend to succeed in the General College program.

The fact that one student makes a percentile score of 98 and another a score of 10 cannot be explained satisfactorily by the amount of time they spend in courses designed to prepare for these tests. Sheer length of exposure to an educational experience seems to bear a very low relationship to actual achievement, for the median correlation between the number of quarter hours of work completed and the scores on comprehensive examinations was .16, the r's for the various comprehensives ranging from .02 to .27.

In contrast to the low relationships discovered between amount of preparatory work and quality of examination performance, there were significant positive relationships between scores on these examinations and the students' ability to deal in verbal symbols, as indicated by intelligence test scores (median $r=.30$) and between these comprehensive examination scores and the high school performance of these students (median $r=.40$). Much more decisive was the relationship existing between these scores and spring-quarter honor-point ratios (median $r=.64$). Although the courses offered in the General College seem to differ fundamentally, in respect to both content and teaching methods, from those given in other divisions of the university, young people distinguished primarily by their verbal aptitude tend to succeed in this general education program as they do in other colleges. The chief difference is that the General College achievement standards are set at a much lower level, permitting more students to pass. This apparently accounts for the fact that the length of time young people stay in the college is unrelated to their general aptitude, although the quality of the work they accomplish definitely does depend on their fundamental verbal ability.

THE KINDS OF STUDENTS WHO RECEIVE DEGREES

As a new degree that has yet to win prestige the Associate in Arts has been awarded to only a small minority of General College students. Of the 1933 entrants, for example, 16 per cent ultimately received this degree, and this proportion decreased to 10 per cent for the entering classes of 1935 and 1937. In each of these three groups about 6 per cent of the students fulfilled all the requirements for graduation but did not apply for the Associate in Arts degree. Because so many more sophomores returned to school in the fall of 1940, the percentage of degrees awarded may be significantly higher in future years. On the whole, however, during the eight-year period surveyed in the present study, less than one student in five who began the General College program successfully completed it.

The kinds of young people on whom a college puts its stamp of approval by awarding its degree or diploma constitute a very interesting test of its own program. Differences between those who receive a degree and those who withdraw from college before graduation reveal how much selection has occurred among those entering the college and on what bases this sorting has taken place. In the General College, students who have actually taken the A.A. degree have been somewhat superior in scholastic ability to those who became eligible for it by fulfilling the comprehensive examination requirements but did not apply for the degree. This latter group could not be distinguished from the general run of entering students in four of the six differences tested. Although the graduates have consistently ranked somewhat higher, the year-by-year fluctuations make an exact statement of their superiority difficult. In the 1933–34 entering class, for example, the group who subsequently received degrees ranked at about the fifty-ninth percentile on these measures. Among the 1935–36 entering students there was very little difference, the rank of the typical graduate falling at about the fifty-fourth percentile. In the 1937–38 group the average percentile rank of graduates was 74, suggesting a much more rigorous selection.

SUMMARY

We must interpret the fact that students remain in the General College for a shorter time than do the students in other colleges of the university in the light of many types of evidence, such as differences in the aims of the various divisions, the reasons why students leave college, and the later activities of those who withdraw. Certainly length of residence alone does not constitute a valid test of the General College program, since the college was established primarily to meet the needs of an increasingly large group for whom a full four-year program was judged unsuitable and hence many students are deliberately counseled to leave college at the end of their freshman year.

Nor is it possible to generalize widely from the courses elected by General College students, although certain facts revealed in this survey, such as the rapid turnover of students in General College courses, hold exceedingly important educational implications. Far more important than the curriculum *on paper* is the curriculum *in students* — the actual changes wrought by these educational experiences in the thinking and living of young people. It is with this problem that the present report is chiefly concerned. In the sections that follow, evidence will be examined to find out to what extent the goals set forth by the General College faculty and the procedures they have used in attempting to attain these goals have actually brought about the desired results.

Readiness for Continued Learning

One purpose in establishing the General College was to provide a kind of laboratory where students of moderate academic ability, or those whose aptitude for extended university work seemed doubtful, could be carefully studied over a period of time. Just which members of such a group should be encouraged to spend the next few years in the academic and professional schools of the university and which should be advised to seek out-of-school opportunities? The problem is a vital one, for although only a small minority of General College students might be expected to take further training, it is important to know whether the most promising young people, from an academic standpoint, are those who have been stimulated to continue their formal education. To appraise fairly this program of general education, therefore, the numbers and types of General College students who have transferred to other divisions of the university or to colleges elsewhere should be known.

Whether or not young people enter other colleges, however, they should all be continuing their education far beyond the period of General College residence. The preparation given by the college for further learning and the kinds of experience of which students avail themselves after leaving the college must therefore constitute searching tests of the worth of the program. In the present study only a beginning could be made in collecting such information, but the results at least suggest the importance of appraising not only their general competence when they leave school but also their readiness for continued learning.

ACQUISITION OF SKILLS FOR CONTINUED LEARNING

General College courses have been especially designed to arouse interests in many everyday problems and to prepare young people to follow these interests both independently and in advanced college work. Certain outcomes of the program discussed in later chapters, such as the scope of students' reading interests and the quality of their insight and understanding, help to show what background or preparation the General College has given for later independent study. The criteria to be discussed in this chapter are two skills, reading and English usage, that seem basic to further learning. Do students improve significantly in these abilities during their stay in the General College, and can any such growth be attributed to their residence in the college? [1]

The Cooperative English Test, composed of sections on usage, spelling, and vocabulary, was used to determine how much students gained in these abilities from the beginning of their freshman year to the end of their sophomore year. As Figure 8 indicates, the typical sophomore advances from his entrance score of 133 to a score of 147; that is, he progresses from a sixteenth percentile on the university norms to a twenty-third percentile — a statistically significant gain. Similar gains were manifested on each of the three separate sections of this test.

The progress made by General College students during this period was then compared with that made by other University of Minnesota students who took the test at entrance and at the end of their sophomore year. Inasmuch as these other groups began at much higher levels of ability and proficiency in English, the scores they achieved by the end of the sophomore year had to be adjusted for the wide differences between them and the General College groups in initial linguistic ability. Using analyses of covariance, which permit correction of final scores for differences in initial status, adjustments were made for differences both in high school rank and in English test scores made at entrance to college.[2] Though all groups gained substantially

[1] Discussion of changes that occur in these particular skills may serve to illustrate how a really comprehensive evaluation of the program might yet be made, utilizing measures of skills, abilities, and interests in the many areas with which general education is concerned.

[2] For a discussion of the technique of covariance analysis see E. F. Lindquist, *Statistical Analysis in Educational Research* (Boston: Houghton Mifflin, 1940), pp. 180–206.

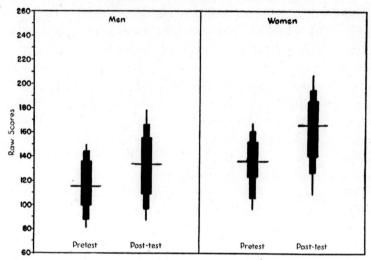

Figure 8. Scores of General College students at entrance and at the end of the sophomore year on the Cooperative English Test. The wide part of each bar represents the range in ratings for the middle half of the students in the designated group. The narrow parts extend to the sixteenth and eighty-fourth percentiles, and the lines at the end extend down to the tenth and up to the ninetieth percentile. The short cross near the middle of each bar indicates the median rating of the group.

during this two-year period, the two populations outside the General College, composed of sophomores in the College of Education and in the College of Science, Literature, and the Arts, made distinctly greater gains than the General College students even when initial differences in ability were taken fully into account. The fact that students outside the General College gained more in these particular skills than General College students did may be due not only to the compulsory English requirements that exist in the two other colleges but to the character of the courses offered. In the General College writing laboratory, emphasis is placed on the reorientation of the students' attitudes toward English, so that they will derive continuing pleasure and satisfaction from expressing themselves effectively, and thus less attention is undoubtedly given to problems of grammar, usage, and composition.

The English achievement scores of General College students who had taken two or more quarters of work in the writing

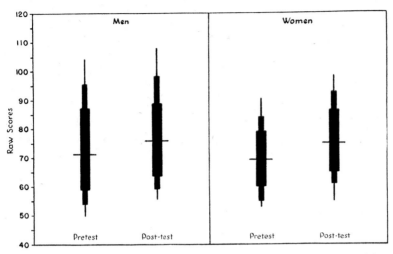

Figure 9. Scores of General College students at entrance and at the end of the sophomore year on the Minnesota Reading Test. (See Figure 8 for explanation.)

laboratory were then compared with those of other General College students in this field, and the scores made by students who had taken Literature Today were compared with those of students not so enrolled. In neither instance were the differences significant, even at the 10 per cent level. These results suggest that the Cooperative English Test may not measure the kinds of outcomes to be expected from these General College courses.[3]

Another basic skill for continued learning in the university and in out-of-school situations is reading. Hence the Minnesota Reading Test was readministered to all sophomores to compare their scores with those they made as entering freshmen. Small gains were revealed for both the men and the women students, the differences between initial and final scores being significant only at the 5 per cent level. The typical sophomore achieved a score equivalent to the sixty-eighth percentile of the entire freshman distribution, as may be seen in Figure 9. Because reading skills are not especially emphasized in any single course, the possible relationship of this gain to various contributing experiences in

[3] In the next chapter are discussed such other outcomes of these courses as reading tastes and scope of literary acquaintance.

the General College could not be determined. Similarly, the absence of test results for students in other colleges made it impossible to trace such gains to maturation, to the university environment as a whole, or to specific General College courses.

PLANS FOR FURTHER EDUCATIONAL WORK

When they entered the General College, it was discovered in this study, only a fourth of the men and two fifths of the women students looked forward to receiving the A.A. degree. As was pointed out in Chapter 4, the majority hoped to earn bachelor's degrees in other units of the university. The fact that more than half of these young people expected to remain in the General College for three quarters or less also indicated that they came to the college primarily to gain entrance into the college of their initial choice rather than to receive a terminal education.

The extent to which young people carry through or modify these expectations during their residence in the General College affords illuminating evidence concerning the guidance and counseling these students received. Were the plans they expressed at the end of their freshman year significantly different from those outlined at the start of their college work? [4] Were these new plans better suited to their demonstrated abilities and interests? It is obviously a matter of opinion just how much alteration or development in immediate or long-range goals should occur as a result of a year spent in college, but comparisons of students' plans outlined at the beginning and at the close of the year may at least suggest whether the direction of change is an appropriate one for them.

According to a study of these comparisons, young people's expectations concerning their length of stay in the General College were considerably altered during their freshman year. As Table 2 shows, seldom did as many as two thirds of the students in any group carry to completion the plans they had outlined when they entered. Two facts revealed in this table, however, are difficult to explain. Students who said that they expected to

[4] Because information concerning educational plans was not included in the freshman blanks until the fall of 1939, it was impossible to study this type of change for a period longer than a single year.

82

remain in the General College for two quarters actually remained for a shorter period than those who planned to stay only one quarter; likewise those who had looked forward to more than three quarters of residence remained for a shorter period than those who had set three quarters as their probable length of stay. Of the freshman class as a whole, 33 per cent of the men and 39 per cent of the women remained for a shorter time than they had planned. The rest either had carried through their original intentions or were in the process of doing so.

TABLE 2. COMPARISON OF STUDENTS' ESTIMATED LENGTH OF STAY WITH THEIR ACTUAL PERIOD OF RESIDENCE IN THE GENERAL COLLEGE (1939–40)

Expected Length of Stay	N	Actual Length of Stay (First Year)			
		One or Two Quarters		Three Quarters	
		Number	Per Cent	Number	Per Cent
One quarter	45	16	35.6	29	64.4
Two quarters	41	31	75.6	10	24.4
Three quarters	316	105	33.3	211	66.7
More than three quarters	192	90	46.9	102	53.1

A greater realism in educational planning is suggested by the replies the students gave at the end of the year to a question concerning their expectations of transferring to some other college. Of all the young people who had indicated in the fall that they hoped to transfer to a specific college, only 38 per cent of the men and 29 per cent of the women still expected to enter that division. Percentages varied widely, however, according to the particular colleges in which these students looked forward to enrolling. More than two thirds of the prospective College of Education students still held to that goal, as against one third of those who had originally intended to enter either the Institute of Technology or the School of Nursing. In other words only a minority of the students held the same educational expectations in the spring of their first year as they had the previous fall. The fact that most changes were in the direction of greater realism constitutes important evidence of the excellent counseling many of them had received.

Significant changes also occurred in plans for obtaining degrees, as may be seen in Figure 10. Outstanding were the decrease in the numbers of those who hoped to receive degrees from the arts college or the Institute of Technology and the increase in the numbers of those who said that they were uncertain about receiving a degree or definitely did not expect one. Almost half of all students who in October had expressed plans for obtain-

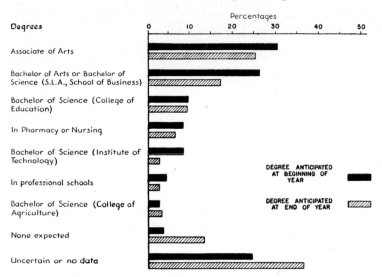

Figure 10. College degrees anticipated by General College students at entrance and at the end of the freshman year.

ing college degrees altered them during the year. If all the young people who dropped out during the year were represented in these tabulations, instead of simply those who outlined plans in both the fall and the spring, these changes would be more impressive.

THE SUCCESS OF TRANSFERRED STUDENTS

Most General College students originally hoped to be admitted to some other college or division of the University of Minnesota for professional training. More than 40 per cent of the 1939–40 freshmen planned to enter the College of Science, Literature, and the Arts, whereas only 14 per cent indicated that they had intended from the start to come to the General College. Twenty-five per cent of the entering freshmen provided no evidence concerning their college plans. Although a decisive majority of those who outlined their educational plans expected to remain only a short time in the General College, as has been pointed out previously, about three fourths of all the entering students hoped to receive degrees from some other division of the university.

Most of those who expected to receive degrees from other colleges, however, faced eventual disappointment. Since this change in plan usually occurred while they were in the General College, many were saved the experience of having to drop out of another college through failure or discouragement. Hence the fact that only a fourth of all entrants during these eight years have transferred from the General College to another division of the university is probably evidence of the realistic counseling General College students receive. Because less than 1 per cent have requested that transcripts of their grades be sent to other institutions, the number who have transferred to colleges or universities elsewhere must also be very small.

The fact that so few students have entered another college or division of the university is also partly due to the increasingly rigorous requirements for transfer students set by agreement between these divisions and the General College. At the present time a General College student is not considered eligible for transfer unless he ranks well above the average of his class in both his course work and his comprehensive examination grades. In the College of Science, Literature, and the Arts, where academic competition is exceedingly keen, the transfer threshold has been raised to the seventy-fifth percentile of the General College distribution. The very existence of such a threshold must bar the majority of students from even applying for transfer to the arts college.

About a third of all the students who have actually been admitted to another division have gone to the College of Science, Literature, and the Arts, as may be seen in Figure 11. The General College counselors' policy of encouraging only the ablest students to apply for transfer to that division undoubtedly accounts for the slight decrease in numbers admitted there in re-

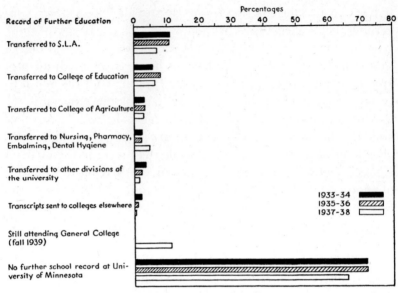

Figure 11. Further college education of students after leaving the General College.

cent years. The College of Education ranks next in the number of transferred students received from the General College. Other transferred students have been rather evenly distributed among the remaining undergraduate divisions of the university.

It is obvious that students whose applications for transfer were accepted by other colleges were a much more select group, academically, than the total group of General College students. As the data in Table 3 indicate, the typical transferred student ranked about ten percentile points higher in his high school achievement

TABLE 3. ACADEMIC APTITUDE AND ACHIEVEMENT OF TRANSFERRED STUDENTS AND STUDENTS WHO DID NOT TRANSFER, IN TERMS OF PERCENTILE RANKS

Entering Classes	High School Rank		College Aptitude Test Rating		Grade-Point Average (Spring)	
	Transferred	Not Transferred	Transferred	Not Transferred	Transferred	Not Transferred
1933–34	41.4	30.0	26.0	21.4	57.3	35.9
1935–36	46.0	31.0	25.4	23.1	64.4	39.5
1937–38	35.7	27.9	21.8	18.0	50.2	35.2

than other General College entrants.[5] In his scholastic achievement in the General College he was distinctly superior, for his honor-point ratio was from twenty to twenty-five percentile points above that of the average General College student. Rather surprisingly, transfer students were not especially distinguished by their performance on the American Council Psychological Examination.

Students who subsequently transferred to other colleges more frequently included courses from these divisions in their General College programs, being in most cases counseled to do so as a kind of try-out or exploratory experience. As might be expected, courses in physical science and in literature, speech, and writing were elected more often by such students, whereas students who took no further work were more often enrolled in the euthenics and general arts courses. The fact that students who received the Associate in Arts degree were no more likely to transfer to other colleges than was the average General College student suggests that the degree has been sought predominantly by those who planned to do no further university work. Those who became eligible for the degree by virtue of passing six comprehensive examinations but did not apply for the degree were more likely to transfer to other colleges; two fifths of this group, as compared with a fourth of the graduates, were transferred.

Though the data in Table 3 show that the General College has been in some measure successful in sorting or distributing students according to their several abilities, there is nevertheless a great deal of overlapping in the abilities of students who do and do not transfer to other colleges. Actually among those students who ranked at the fiftieth percentile in their high school graduating class or their college aptitude test performance, the larger proportion did not transfer to other units.

Among students who were above average in their high school work, one in every three of those who entered during the year 1935–36 subsequently transferred to another college; among

[5] All percentile scores used in the present study were transmuted into standard scores for purposes of analysis and then reconverted to percentile form in order to facilitate interpretation of results.

1937–38 entrants three out of every seven students who achieved at this level transferred to another college. This fact suggests that the abler students have recently been given more encouragement to continue their college work. It is still true, however, that a good many students of low academic promise transfer to other units, despite the fact that the odds are strongly against their successfully completing the new program.

Although the group who transferred were among the more academically able General College students they did not, on the whole, succeed too well in their subsequent work. The average number of quarters that they remained in the unit to which they transferred was only four—obviously far too short a time to complete the new programs. Furthermore, of all those who transferred during this eight-year period, slightly less than half either received degrees from other colleges or were still in school at the time this study was made. In general, therefore, we may say that one person out of every eight or nine students who enter the General College is likely to complete a liberal arts or a professional school program. This apparently low percentage can easily be misinterpreted if two facts are not borne in mind—first, that many General College students lack the interest and the ability to do extended university work; second, that even in the most selective liberal arts colleges, half the students usually fail to complete the program. Hence, far from indicating inadequacy or failure on the part of the General College staff, these figures suggest an unusually good salvage job.

ATTITUDES OF TRANSFERRED STUDENTS

Since students who have transferred to other colleges have had more opportunities than other students to test the preparation that the General College has given them for continued learning in a college or university, they were asked to make certain comparisons between their General College courses and their present study programs in the academic and professional colleges. Responses to a questionnaire sent to the students who had transferred to other colleges during a two-year period (1938–40) were received from approximately two thirds of all the young people queried. One hundred and ten questionnaires were returned by transferred students who were still in school, and 48 more by students who had recently withdrawn from the colleges to which they had transferred.

One of the first problems investigated was that of methods of instruction. Were some techniques used more often in the Gen-

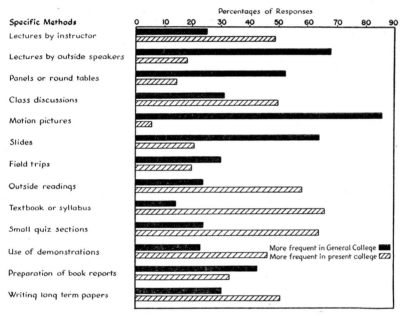

Figure 12. Comparisons made by transferred students of instructional methods used in the General College and in other colleges in which they subsequently enrolled.

eral College than in other divisions, and vice versa? From a check list covering a great many university teaching practices, students selected those most characteristic of the colleges in which they had been enrolled. As may be seen in Figure 12, motion pictures, lectures by outside speakers, slides, and panels or round-table discussions were much more common in the General College; textbooks or syllabi, small quiz sections, outside readings, long papers, and class discussions were mentioned as being used more often in the other colleges. These marked differences in methods, combined with differences in the actual content of courses, naturally lead one to expect pronounced differences in educational outcomes. Differences in instructional techniques also deserve study since they may conceivably influence the type of preparation afforded by General College courses for work in other divisions of the university.

The relative amount of time spent in preparation for General College courses and present courses was also studied. Students expressed their judgments by checking the appropriate phrase on

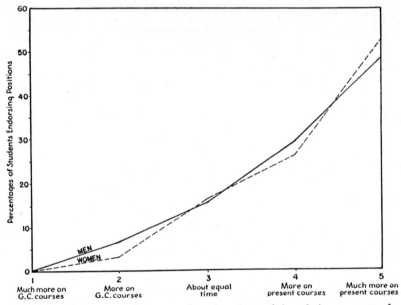

Figure 13. Estimates made by transferred students of the relative amounts of study time spent on General College courses and on their present courses.

a five-point scale ranging from *much more time spent on General College courses* to *much more time spent on present courses.* By an overwhelming vote these young people indicated that their present courses demanded more of their time (Figure 13). No student, for example, said that he had spent *much more time* on General College courses, and only 5 per cent of the total group of transferred students said they had devoted *more time* to those courses. In contrast, 28 per cent said that they were spending *more time* on their present courses, and almost 50 per cent said these courses demanded *much more time*. More than three fourths of the transferred students, therefore, had found that the courses in which they were now enrolled required considerably more time and effort. Of course these students, having left the General College after one or two years, were often doing upper-class work, which normally demands more intensive study than freshman or sophomore courses do. Although this is undoubtedly one factor, however, it does not seem to explain adequately the marked differences in the demands made by the two types of programs.

Evaluations of specific General College courses were also obtained from these students. Since these will be presented in Chapter 11, in connection with students' attitudes toward the curriculum, discussion here will be restricted to the values of these courses in further university work. The courses most definitely helpful, in the opinion of students who transferred to other units, were, in the order mentioned, Human Biology, Business Mathematics, Practical Applications of Psychology, American Citizen and His Government, Oral Communication, and Physical Science. These judgments were based, it must be remembered, on the demands made by continued college work rather than on the out-of-school usefulness of the materials learned. The questionnaire responses simply show that transferred students attach the most value to broad subject-matter survey courses and to the instruction in speech.

Transferred students were particularly appreciative of the assistance they had received from General College counselors and faculty advisers. More than 80 per cent of them were aware of receiving definite help. This was related principally to the clarification of educational and vocational plans, although many students acknowledged specific assistance with study problems or problems arising from personal and family difficulties.

In answer to a final question students expressed their present attitudes toward General College work as preparation for further university study. On the five-point scale provided for the expression of these opinions approximately the same percentages of students (one in every twelve) checked the extreme positions, *should be recommended to all students* and *a waste of time — of no real help.* Only 15 per cent checked the middle position, *about the same value as other college work.*[6] The students who favored the General College program as preparation for later work (39 per cent) outnumbered those who considered it less valuable than work elsewhere might have been (26 per cent). In other words, these former General College students were favorably inclined toward the program, since almost two thirds of the group believed that the training they had received in the General College was at least equal in value to what they might have obtained elsewhere in the same period of time. When we recall that a great many young people did not come to the General College by their own choice, this belief seems to represent a more definite endorsement of the program than might have been expected.

FURTHER EDUCATIONAL ACTIVITIES OF OTHER STUDENTS

Students who had not transferred to some other division of the university were also questioned, to determine whether they had taken any college or vocational courses since leaving the General College, whether they were now attending some type of school, and whether they planned to return to school at any time in the future. It appeared from the replies that students who had recently withdrawn were quite optimistic concerning their chances of reentering the university.[7] More than a third of them expected to be back in school the following year, a hope actually fulfilled for only 10 per cent of the group, which included a few more men than women students. Those who returned also tended to be among the more able students.

A very small number of those who had lately dropped out of

[6] The only significant difference between the attitudes expressed on this point by students who transferred and were still in school and those who transferred but subsequently withdrew was that those who dropped out tended to be more neutral in their attitude (28 per cent taking the middle position and the others clustered at the points immediately above and below the center of the scale), indicating that they did not feel that enrollment in the General College made much difference.

[7] The findings are based on the replies of 310 students who withdrew from the General College in 1938–40, and 253 students who had withdrawn earlier. The samples used were entirely representative of the young people served by the General College.

the General College seemed to be availing themselves of other school opportunities. One former General College student in every fifteen reported that he was attending some type of school, usually a vocational institution such as a trade school or business college. An occasional student had entered a junior college or liberal arts college elsewhere or was taking apprentice training in industry. A few students mentioned courses, either cultural or vocational, that they were taking in the university extension or correspondence divisions.

Among students who had been out of college from three to seven years a great deal more training was reported. Out of every ten former students, only three said that they had had no further education of any sort. By far the largest number — four in every ten — had gone to a business school or a technical institute of some type, a fact furnishing an interesting corroboration of students' predominant concern, while in college, with problems of vocational choice and job readiness. Two out of every ten had taken some additional courses at the University of Minnesota, or at another college, and one student in ten indicated that this further work, usually vocational, had been done at night school or through correspondence courses. Without comparable data for other students of similar abilities and interests it is impossible to say whether general education has really given these students a more intense desire for continued training than they might have gained in another college. The data do indicate, however, that because the additional training received is primarily vocational, the more formal general education of most students is completed in the General College.

SUMMARY

For the vast majority of its students, then, the General College provides the last systematic educational orientation that they will receive before facing all the problems of vocational adjustment, social relationships, and responsible citizenship that await them outside the classroom. What is not done in this final period of education will often remain undone. For those students who will transfer to some other institution the present findings suggest that the General College ought to provide more thorough preparation in basic study skills. The results likewise emphasize the need for more satisfactory criteria of readiness for further study at the university level, so that qualified students may be encouraged to continue their college work. Also needed are penetrating studies of the learning problems encountered by former General College students in the colleges to which they transfer. Since we still know very little about the values of broad survey or orientation courses as preparation for more advanced work, the results of such studies would have important implications for the whole field of general education. Finally, for the benefit of all students — those who transfer to other full-time programs, those who enroll for part-time courses, and those who take no further work — there ought to be a thorough study of both the stimulation and the preparation such courses provide for the learning that must continue throughout life.

CHAPTER 7

Orientation to Personal Living

One of the most vigorously endorsed aims of the General College program has been to develop in the student an understanding of his own drives, abilities, interests, and goals, so that, recognizing the pattern of his strengths and weaknesses, he may enter more actively and fully into the life about him. The General College counseling service and the special courses planned to help young people to attain physical and mental health and to broaden and enrich their social relationships indicate how genuinely the whole staff has been concerned with their students' growth in self-understanding and self-direction. Because of the importance of these objectives and the effort devoted to their attainment, many different types of evidence were gathered that might help to reveal the contribution of the General College program to this area.

Thus an effort was made to probe students' understanding of factors influencing wholesome adjustment, their actual success in working out happy family and social relationships, the breadth of their avocational interests, and their own appraisal of how they had developed personally during their one or two years in the General College.

UNDERSTANDING OF PERSONAL ADJUSTMENT PROBLEMS

Does a young person who has spent months or years in the General College acquire deeper insight into his personal problems? Does he understand more clearly the basic facts of psychology, biology, and sociology that underlie intelligent personal and social adjustment? A knowledge of such facts is undoubtedly much less significant than his application of this knowledge to his own adjustment; still, since we cannot follow him from day to day for a significant period of time to find out how well he is making this application, it has seemed essential to determine how much his understanding of such problems is increased during his residence in the college.

Because this appraisal began simultaneously with the establishment of the individual orientation area, which was primarily concerned with developing such understanding, tests paralleling the materials included in these particular courses were not ready for administration until the next year, the fall of 1939. Giving these tests to all students in the college at the beginning and the end of that academic year yielded a one-year measure of growth.

Two forms of a so-called Personal Living Test, designed to measure fundamental facts and generalizations concerning personal adjustment, were developed, with the full cooperation of the faculty.[1] These tests required 45 minutes each and were equated, in so far as existent item analyses permitted, with respect to the difficulty and character of the items used. When administered in early October as a pretest for all students in the General College, they yielded reliability coefficients of .83 (Form A) and .85 (Form B), these correlations being based on the scores of entering freshmen exclusively. At the end of the year the tests were given again, this time yielding reliability coefficients of .83 (Form A) and .91 (Form B).[2] Illustrative items are reproduced below:

In a home situation where there is continual friction with domineering parents usually the best thing for an older adolescent to do is to (1) walk out, (2) stick up for his rights to the last ditch, (3) analyze the points of conflict and adjust to them temporarily, (4) try to make the parents see his way of thinking, (5) pretend he is sick so that they will feel sorry for him.

[1] The procedures used in developing these informational tests are described in Ruth E. Eckert and C. Robert Pace, "A Cooperative Appraisal," *Journal of Higher Education*, 13:33–38.

[2] For this spring testing the students were so arranged by Fisher's Random Numbers that half of them repeated the same form taken in the fall and the other half took the alternative form. It was thus possible to investigate through covariance analyses the effect of the particular form of the test taken on the students' achievement. Since no significant differences, even at the 5 per cent level, appeared in the achievement of the four groups (those who took AA, AB, BA, or BB) it was possible to disregard the form of the test, or the particular combination of tests used, in all later studies of the outcomes of the individual orientation area.

Men and women differ mainly because women (1) tend to be far more sensitive, (2) have more intuition, (3) have been expected to engage in different activities, (4) are less able mentally, (5) are inferior physically.

A high school graduate discovers that his college ability equals that of only the lowest 10 per cent of high school seniors. He wants to enter law because several friends of the family have achieved marked financial success in that field. Probably the best step for him to take would be to (1) enroll in a prelegal course, (2) enter medicine or engineering rather than law, (3) realize that he will be successful in only the lowest unskilled trades, (4) give up the idea of entering professional work, (5) try to increase his intelligence by persistent work in college.

The best of the following arguments for taking up music as a hobby is that it (1) enables one to appear before people and win their applause, (2) enables one to meet more people, (3) gives one a great deal of personal satisfaction, (4) will make it possible for one to earn extra money later on, (5) is a hobby most of one's friends are taking up.

As Figure 14 shows, students in the orientation course possessed superior understanding in this field, even before they had had any special instruction. This was the only area, as later chapters will show, in which those enrolled in one of the so-called functional-need courses were differentiated at the outset of their work from those who did not take the course. Interestingly enough, the students who were seemingly in most need of such instruction were those who did not take the course. This figure also shows that sophomores who had taken the core course the preceding year began their second year's work in the General College at about the same level of understanding as that attained by the present freshmen at the end of the year.

Whether or not the freshmen were enrolled in the Individual Orientation course, which had been particularly designed to develop these understandings, they gained so much knowledge of this type during the year that the score attained by the typical freshman at the end of the year corresponded to the seventy-fifth percentile score for students tested at the beginning of the year. From these results it would appear that the whole curriculum and advisory service contribute to the same ends as the special

97

course, Individual Orientation, does. This end-of-the-year performance of General College freshmen was also very similar to
the achievement of a representative group of Science, Literature,
and Arts freshmen who had taken the same test in the fall.[3]

From the data presented in Figure 14, then, it appears that, as
far as a knowledge of facts was concerned, there was no special
advantage to be gained from taking the Individual Orientation

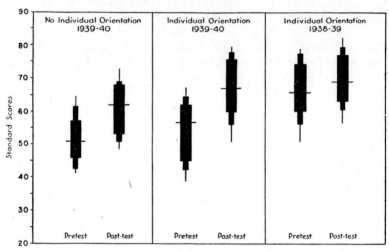

Figure 14. Scores of students who had taken the Individual Orientation course
and those who had not on the Personal Living Test. The scale used in charting
these results is based on standard scores derived from the scores of all entering
freshmen on these tests. A score of 50 thus represents typical performance,
and 40 or 60 the achievement of students who ranked one standard deviation
below or above the mean. (See Figure 8 for explanation.)

course. Students who did not take such a course scored almost as
high at the end of the year as those who did. When more precise
comparisons were made, however, using covariance techniques
that permitted adjustment of final scores on this test for differences in initial scores and in high school percentile rank, those

[3] Representative students in three colleges — Science, Literature, and the Arts;
Education; Agriculture, Forestry, and Home Economics — had been invited to
take these tests as part of an experimental study. They responded in sufficient
numbers (S.L.A., 113 students; Education, 127 students; and Agriculture, Forestry, and Home Economics, 107 students) to permit interesting comparisons with
General College results. Because of the relatively high initial scores made by
students from other colleges, the original plan of readministering the tests to
these students at the end of the year was not carried through.

who were enrolled in the course for two or three quarters gained significantly more than other students. The F-ratio was 10.76, though a ratio of only 3.83 was required to meet the 1 per cent level of significance. A systematic effort to teach directly certain of the necessary understandings had thus been attended by some degree of success.

Although General College sophomores made much higher scores than freshmen at the beginning of the year, covariance analyses revealed that they still gained relatively as much as the first-year students did. This again suggests that the program as a whole operates to develop and reinforce these types of understanding. Likewise men students made as large strides as the women did in acquiring the kinds of information and understanding measured by this particular test. These analyses included all freshmen and sophomores who took both tests, whether or not they were enrolled in the Individual Orientation course that year. This explains the seeming divergence from the distribution of scores given in Figure 14, for here the sophomore group was restricted to students who had taken the course the preceding year.

An examination measuring the more specialized factual information included in the Individual Orientation core course was constructed by Nicholas A. Fattu, director of a special investigation of this area sponsored by the University Committee on Educational Research. As has been shown in his report, students enrolled in the core course made significantly greater advances than other students in learning the more technical vocabulary of psychology, important laws or principles, and the basic methodology for studying human behavior.[4] In Fattu's analysis all General College students were sectioned into eight groups: those who had not taken Individual Orientation; those who had taken Individual Orientation, Practical Applications of Psychology, or Human Development and Personal Adjustment — the three courses that seemed to overlap most; and those who had taken the various possible combinations of those courses. The superior-

---

[4] Nicholas A. Fattu, "Evaluation Program in Individual Orientation," in the *Biennial Report of the University Committee on Educational Research, 1938–40* (Minneapolis: University of Minnesota, 1941), pp. 108–30.

ity of the Individual Orientation course, taken alone or in combination with other courses, in building this kind of knowledge is clearly demonstrated in Fattu's report. It may be said in summary, then, that results from both a broad-gauged test of the knowledge and understandings developed in this area and from a more restricted test of specialized information attest to the importance of a course in individual orientation in developing these types of outcomes.

ADEQUACY OF PERSONAL ADJUSTMENT

Even more important than the knowledge he gains about himself and other people may be the quality of the student's social adjustments. Thus in the outline of General College goals given in Chapter 3, many statements relate to the student's sense of personal well-being and the ease with which he can meet problems of health, family relationships, work adjustments, and leisure-time associations. Results obtained from personality tests hence afford another kind of evidence for the appraisal both of the General College program as a whole and of those courses that have been specifically planned to assist young people in meeting their personal adjustment problems.

The Minnesota Personality Scale, which was constructed on the basis of factor analyses of current personality tests, yields measures of adjustment in five areas: morale, social adjustment, family relations, emotionality, and economic conservatism. The gains that men freshmen made in these types of adjustment during their first year in the General College are set forth in Figure 15; those of the women are given in Figure 16. The most striking fact revealed by these two figures is the relatively small change that occurs in the adjustment scores attained by the typical or average student during one year. Scores on only two sections, Morale and Social Adjustment, reveal changes that are too large to be due to chance fluctuations in measurement. The real loss that appears on the morale scale, reflecting the individual's conception of his own worth, may perhaps be attributed to a certain amount of "downgrading," or counseling toward greater realism, that teachers and counselors must promote because of the

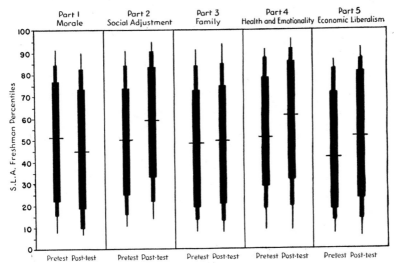

Figure 15. Fall and spring scores of General College men on the Minnesota Personality Scale. Since different scales were employed for each of the five sections, the scores of General College students were plotted against S.L.A. percentile values in order to present the results on one chart. The vertical distances are not comparable because a percentile rather than a sigma scale was used. Distances in the middle of the scale are therefore less significant than those near the ends. In order that the top of the scale may uniformly represent desired characteristics, scores on Part 5 have been so treated that higher scores represent increasing liberalism instead of conservatism, as they did in the original test. (See Figure 8 for explanation.)

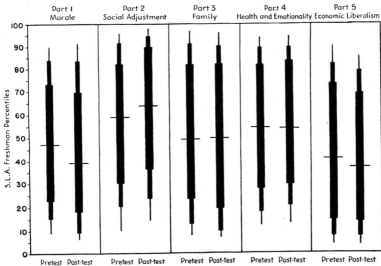

Figure 16. Fall and spring scores of General College women on the Minnesota Personality Scale. (See Figures 8 and 15 for explanation.)

overambitious educational and vocational plans expressed by many students. In other words, this particular loss should perhaps be interpreted as an actual gain.

The gain shown on the social adjustment section is all the more impressive because General College students made higher initial scores than the arts college students did on this section, as may be seen in Figures 15 and 16. On the Family and the Health and Emotionality sections the changes are insignificant for the sexes combined, although for the men alone the gain on the latter section approaches significance. On the Economic Liberalism section the conflict between results for the men students, who became more liberal, and those for the women students, who tended to become more conservative, render it questionable that these latter changes can be attributed to General College residence.

When the scores attained by General College students on Section II, Social Adjustment, where the largest gain was shown, were compared with those made by College of Education sophomores who had taken the test at the same time, it was found that the students in the College of Education had reached almost the same end-of-the-year level as General College students. More precise comparisons — using covariance techniques that permitted adjustment for the large differences between the groups in high school achievement and college aptitude test results — likewise indicated no significant differences in the amount both groups gained. The gain made by General College young people in social adjustment can therefore hardly be attributed to distinctive features in the General College program.

Since the results obtained from the Minnesota Personality Scale had been studied by Fattu to determine what effect the Individual Orientation course (taken singly or in combination with related courses) had had upon these types of personal and social adjustment, his findings may be briefly summarized here. Not only did he discover no value in this special course for promoting better personal adjustment, as measured by the test, but he found that the women students registered in the Individual Orientation core course actually seemed somewhat more poorly adjusted at the end of the year than they had been at the beginning. Two other personal adjustment inventories, a statement test and an adjectives test, constructed by Fattu for this special appraisal, also corroborated this unexpected and highly disconcerting finding. Judged by these tests the Individual Orientation course does not seem to be effective in furthering personal adjustment goals. As Fattu concludes in his report, "If one were to judge the value of the core course in Individual Orientation in terms of purely informational outcomes, it could be said to have achieved in some measure its aims. If, however, it were to be evaluated in terms of adjustment outcomes as measured in this investigation, one would have to conclude that there was no evidence that students who had taken the course had profited significantly in personal adjustment." [5]

Another test used to discover how much the adjustment of these students improved during their stay in the General College was the Bell Adjustment Inventory, which yields measures of adjustment in four areas — social adjustment, home, health, and emotional adjustment. Since this test had been included in the freshman entrance program, repetition at the end of the sophomore year made possible a study of changes over this two-year period. Significant gains were evident in two sections of this test, Social Adjustment and Emotional Adjustment, as is shown in Figure 17. To what degree young people might have increased their scores on these particular sections if they had simply lived a year or two longer outside any special college environment is of course not known. Without such a control group, about all that may be concluded from the present results is that as sophomores General College students give greater promise of attaining well-adjusted adulthood than they did when they entered college. Because the test was readministered only to sophomores and the number of cases was therefore quite limited, the results were not analyzed on the basis of the presence or absence of the Individual Orientation course.

When students who had been out of college from three to seven years were asked whether any General College courses

[5] *Ibid.*, p. 130.

had helped them to understand better their own personal and emotional problems and to meet them more successfully, almost half of those who had received the Associate in Arts degree (46 per cent) and a third of those who had dropped out (32 per cent) acknowledged such assistance. The course most often mentioned as being of distinct assistance was Psychology, men-

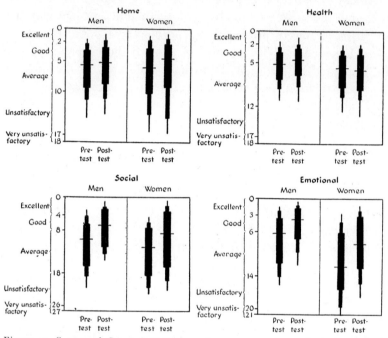

Figure 17. Scores of General College students at entrance and at the end of the sophomore year on the Bell Adjustment Inventory. (See Figure 8 for explanation.)

tioned by 67 students among the 253 who replied; next in order of value seemed to be the courses in Human Development (14 students) and Human Biology (11 students). Other courses received a smattering of votes. It must be remembered that these particular students had been out of college for some time and hence had had no contact with Individual Orientation, the new course designed to promote these outcomes. Among young people who believed that General College courses had definitely promoted personal understanding and adjustment, the following comments were typical:

"Psychology. Merely the study of behavior gave me a clearer insight into other people's problems, and I was able to transfer those problems and solutions to my life."

"Psychology. Because it gave me a better understanding of my personal and emotional problems. I worried less about them, and the course aided me in overcoming to some extent the influence of too much family domination."

"Especially Human Development. Writing down my own analysis of myself and separating the truth from my rationalizing taught me to strive for my real and true self."

"Human Biology. Helped me in a way to differentiate habits."

"Human Development taught me the naturalness of human behavior and how to cope with emotional problems. The course taught me self-confidence and understanding of myself and others. Psychology also helped along this line."

"Psychology gave an answer to any emotional irregularities that seem so unusual but are quite normal."

HEALTH KNOWLEDGE AND ATTITUDES

From the very start of the General College program there has been continuing concern for students' health. One evidence of this has been the development of a three-quarter course in Human Biology taught by a physician. As the data in Chapter 11 indicate, Human Biology has been perhaps the most popular single course in the whole curriculum. Present and former students enthusiastically point out the many values they have acquired from their work in this area. The development of adequate health knowledge and wholesome health attitudes has also been stressed in other areas, particularly in such courses as Individual Orientation and Home Life Orientation. The counseling service, too, has devoted considerable attention to these objectives.

Unfortunately it was impossible within the resources of the present study to investigate the actual effect on student health of the focusing of teaching and counseling efforts upon such objectives. Only fragmentary evidences could be collected, which indirectly suggest the contribution that instruction in this area makes to health knowledge and health habits. On a health-information test constructed at the university and administered to all men students eligible for selective service, the performance of the small group of General College students who took the test equaled that of men enrolled in the College of Science, Literature, and the Arts, despite the striking superiority of the latter students in academic ability.

When the health practices of former General College students were compared with those of young people trained in the usual arts program,[6] General College young people showed definite advantages on every point considered. For example, differences beyond the 1 per cent level of significance were discovered on such practices as paying hospital dues, taking regular physical exercise, and planning for medical and dental care. Students from other colleges manifested more interest than did General College students in finding out about the structure of the human body and how the body works, but this may be because these topics had been extensively treated in the Human Biology course.

When former General College students were asked to state whether any of their courses had helped them to develop better health habits and attitudes and if so to specify the courses that had given them such aid, affirmative answers were received by almost the same proportions of graduates and nongraduates (39 per cent of those who received the Associate in Arts degree and 34 per cent of those who had dropped out). Human Biology was the course almost always specified in answering this question (by 70 students, as compared with 15 for Physical Education, 13 for Psychology, and a few scattered endorsements for other courses). In the students' own language, these are the chief

[6] Pace, *They Went to College*, p. 18ff. Information was obtained from former General College students by means of a sixteen-page illustrated questionnaire modeled after the Pace questionnaire and including many of the same items, so that direct comparisons of results might be made. The questionnaire was completed by 253 former students who had been carefully selected as representative of the group. Both graduates and nongraduates were included. In order to allow for differences in academic ability and lapse of time after leaving college, comparisons were made with arts college students who had dropped out of college after one or two years' work, and who had been out of college only five years.

values that have resulted from General College instruction in the area of personal health:

"Human Biology. From it I learned some preventive measures; much functional information about which I knew absolutely nothing previously. Would like to have learned more about value of advertised patent medicines."

"Human Biology and Dr. O'Brien's course on health. Learning about the structure and functions of the body made me conscious of the necessary care the body must have."

"The gym course showed how my health and body compared with a large group the same age as myself. I have improved since then."

"Human Biology, Human Development, and Personal Adjustment. Helped me because they gave me facts about healthful living, and examples which are a definite proof. They have also instilled the idea of periodic physical examinations."

"I think the course that helped me most was Food Purchase. It has definitely helped me to pick out the better foods for food value and nourishment, as well as to economize in doing so."

"Three quarters of Human Biology. I had never taken any biology before, and each quarter taught me a great deal, with the result I am ever conscious of my own health as well as that of the community and country in which I live."

RECREATIONAL INTERESTS AND ACTIVITIES

What young people do with their free time, both when they are alone and when they are members of social groups, is of considerable concern, since wholesome recreational activities presage good job adjustments as well as happy personal relationships. Partly for this reason the General College has developed several courses in literature, art, music, drama, and photography and has emphasized throughout its program the desirability of cultivating hobbies and satisfying leisure-time pursuits.

Because most of the reading done by adults is confined to newspapers and magazines, the kinds of periodicals read by students now in school and by former students were carefully investigated. At the beginning and at the end of each year, students listed the magazines that they regularly read, and these were then coded according to the Morgan and Leahy scale to

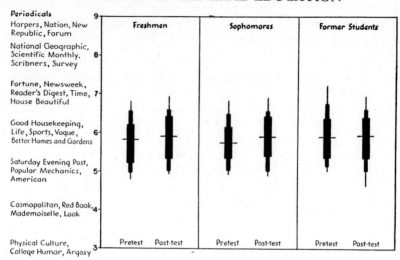

Figure 18. Magazine-reading interests of General College students and General College alumni as shown by average scale values for individuals.

discover changes in reading tastes.[7] Apparently, as Figure 18 shows, very little alteration occurred, the small gain manifested in the quality of the reported magazine reading being no greater than what might be attributed to chance. Likewise there was no significant difference between freshmen and sophomores in the types of magazines they said that they read regularly during the school year. Not a single difference met the 5 per cent level of significance; a rough trend merely pointed toward more reading of *Look* and the *Reader's Digest* by freshmen and more reading of *Time* and the *Cosmopolitan* by sophomores. On the whole the magazine reading done by these General College students would seem to be rather harmless but certainly lacking in the literary and cultural values measured by the Morgan-Leahy scale. Nor does the number of magazines read regularly tend to increase during college residence. When students leave the General College they still read about three magazines each month, women students reporting more magazine titles than do the men students.

Data obtained from former General College students, who re-

[7] W. Morgan and A. Leahy, "Cultural Content of General Interest Magazines," *Journal of Educational Psychology*, 25:530–36.

ported the magazine reading that they were doing after several years out of school, are also summarized in this chart. Since they read about the same quality of periodicals as the young people now in school, it would appear that present General College students will obtain their adult world views, in so far as these come from reading, from the *Reader's Digest*, the *Saturday Evening Post*, *Collier's*, *Life*, *Time*, *Liberty*, and the *Ladies' Home Journal*. A few interesting differences occur, however, between the magazine-reading tastes of present and former students. For example, students still in school read *Time* and *Newsweek* more frequently than the former students — a difference due undoubtedly to the use of *Time* as a text in the large Current History class. The other two magazines read more frequently by students now in school are *Life* and the *Woman's Home Companion*. Among former students more interest was shown in *Better Homes and Gardens*, the *American*, *Good Housekeeping*, and *McCall's*. In both groups fewer than one person in twenty read such magazines as *Harpers*, the *Atlantic Monthly*, the *National Geographic*, the *Saturday Review of Literature*, or the *New Republic*.

The amount of book reading done by present and former students also falls somewhat below what might have been expected. For example, 34 per cent of the men and 16 per cent of the women had read fewer than five books during the year. On the average, twelve books were read each year. Yet 12 per cent of these supposedly nonacademic students said that they had read twenty or more books of fiction and nonfiction during the year. The fact that freshmen and sophomores reported almost identical book titles suggests that an additional year of work in the General College had not measurably affected their reading preferences.

When the titles of books read by present and former students were compared, it was found that young people still in school were more likely to read such current best-sellers as *The Grapes of Wrath*, *Johnny Got His Gun*, and *Gone with the Wind* than were the former students — possibly because these books were discussed in the Literature Today course. Books read somewhat more often by students who had left school were likewise popular recent novels: *Rebecca, My Son, My Son,* and *All This and Heaven Too.* Those students who had completed the general education program and received the A.A. degree were not differentiated in their reported reading, with respect either to the number of books they read or to their quality, from those who had dropped out. When former students, both graduates and nongraduates, were given an opportunity to check the kinds of books they most liked to read, they gave top ranking to books dealing with personalities, travel, and psychological problems and indicated least interest in books about art, hobbies, philosophy, and politics.

Studies of the recreational or free-time social participation of these young people were based on their own reports, which of course might not correspond exactly to their actual activities. The fact that fall and spring reports, as well as those given by freshman and sophomore students, were in close agreement nevertheless suggests that students made reasonably careful estimates of how they used their leisure time. Apparently, very little change in recreational interests occurred during a year of residence in the General College, as may be seen in Table 4. Activities popular at the beginning of the year still held top rank at the end; those that were least popular remained so, with few exceptions. Among sixty-five activities, changes significant at the I per cent level were discovered for only fifteen items.[8] The gains that did occur were largely in sports, physical exercise, and social activities of an informal type. Several of these statistically significant changes bore little direct relationship to the General College curriculum — for example, the greater emphasis at the end of the year on adjusting wiring around the house, engaging in water sports, or selling in a retail store. Of course, a year may

[8] A specially constructed Recreational Interest Questionnaire was used in canvassing the free-time activities of General College students. The student was to indicate the extent of his participation by encircling the appropriate item on a five-point scale, of which the two extremes were *a great deal — far beyond the typical high school graduate* and *rarely or never.* By chi-square techniques it was possible to compare the extent and participation of various student groups at the beginning and end of the year.

TABLE 4. TYPES OF OUT-OF-SCHOOL ACTIVITIES IN WHICH STUDENTS SHOWED GREATEST AND LEAST GAINS DURING ONE YEAR OF RESIDENCE IN THE GENERAL COLLEGE

GREATEST GAINS	LEAST GAINS
(All differences significant at the 1 per cent level)	(No differences significant, even at the 20 per cent level)
1. Bull sessions (largest change)	1. Reading newspapers (no change)
2. Parties without dancing	2. Reading popular story magazines
3. General conversation	3. Reading poetry
4. Competition in tennis, golf, etc.	4. Games carried on alone
5. Games involving mental skill	5. Reading news magazines
6. Telling jokes to a group	6. Writing personal letters
7. Making pencil and crayon drawings	7. Soliciting advertising for school papers
8. Painting	8. Collecting stamps
9. Engaging in water sports	9. Reading novels
10. Attending dramatic productions	10. Listening to plays on the radio
11. Sculpture	11. Listening to radio news commentators
12. Leading discussions in a group	12. Chemistry or physics experiments at home
13. Selling in a retail store	13. Acting as chairman of important committee
14. Fraternity and sorority activities	14. Studying architecture
15. Adjusting wiring around the house	15. Visiting art galleries

be far too short a time for patterns of living outside the school to be significantly changed by any educational program. It is cause for concern, however, when young people's out-of-school activities fail to reveal the immediate impact of an educational experience that has been especially designed to promote participation in home, school, and community living.

In connection with this study of recreational pursuits, entering students listed in the fall and again in the spring all the clubs or associations of which they were members. At the end of the year, as at its beginning, most students reported affiliations with three or four clubs, chiefly of a social type. A substantial minority assumed leadership in these organizations, for one fifth of the boys and one third of the girls reported that they held offices of various types, including committee chairmanships.

More extensive studies were made of the club activities of students who had left or been graduated from the General College in earlier years. More than a fourth (27 per cent) of those who had received the Associate in Arts degree and a sixth (17 per cent) of those who had dropped out indicated no membership in clubs or associations. Those who specified some activity usually listed two or three groups. Church and social betterment organizations, which were mentioned by a fourth of these young adults, led the list, whereas civic and political clubs ranked lowest, involving fewer than one person in every twelve.

The particular kinds of clubs to which these young adults belonged provided some picture of their interests and social attitudes. Labor union memberships, specified by seventeen former students out of the 253 in this group who returned the questionnaire, headed the category of business, labor, and professional organizations. On the other hand, not a single former General College student listed membership in any professional association. Golf clubs, listed by seven students, topped the hobby category, whereas bridge clubs, specified by thirty-five students, ranked first among purely social organizations. Various college fraternities and sororities, mentioned by thirty-nine men and women, were an easy first among fraternal organizations. The Masonic Order, for example, was listed by only five of these young people. The 107 members of church and social betterment groups belonged chiefly to churches, church societies, and Sunday school groups. Among civic and political societies the Young Republicans claimed first place with sixteen memberships, and the Junior Chamber of Commerce ranked second, with four. Study groups of any sort were notably missing from these lists of clubs and organizations. On the whole it does not appear likely that the groups and associations to which these young people voluntarily belong will carry far forward the work that the college has begun.

A special effort was made to discover how much use General College students were making of the rich extracurricular resources for general education available on the university campus. Unfortunately there were no comparable figures for students in the other colleges, so the data presented here must be interpreted in the light of what was expected rather than what other students have done. The campus activity most often reported was attendance at the newsreel theater, patronized by a fifth of students every week and by half of them every other week. The weekly university convocations were attended regularly by less than 15 per cent of the group, though another 50 per cent went once or twice a month. Dances ranked next, about 40 per cent attending at least one or two each quarter. About 3 per cent went regularly to either the music listening hours or the student forums; 60 per cent never attended the listening hours, and 70 per cent never attended the forums. However, since no more than 200 of the 15,000 university students ordinarily attend a given forum meeting or listening hour, the General College group may be displaying a more active interest than these statistics suggest. About 20 per cent were attracted to exhibits at the university gallery, principally those showing abstract, primitive, or contemporary American art. Only 7 per cent of the students were present at any session of the conference on "Democracy — Today and Tomorrow"; 5 per cent attended at least one of the four Sigma Xi lectures on recent medical developments; less than 2 per cent took part in the Pan-American conferences held on the campus during the year.

Seldom did more than one out of ten General College young people attend dramatic or musical events at the university, such as concerts by the Minneapolis Symphony Orchestra or by soloists, or plays at the University of Minnesota studio theater, or go to plays downtown. If more than 10 per cent reported attendance at any of these performances, some glamorous, well-advertised feature was usually involved — Lily Pons and André Kostelanetz, Alec Templeton, Donald Dixon, Nelson Eddy, all radio or movie stars. In the long lists of motion picture titles reported there was little evidence that these young people had made an effort to select unusual pictures or those of pronounced artistic merit, for the productions most of them saw were *Scarface, Zola, It Happened One Night* — all former box-office movies with stars; *Romeo and Juliet, Tobacco Road, Gone with the Wind* — productions that they might feel under obligation to see.

Among radio programs, preference for variety, comedy, and popular music predominated both at the beginning and at the end of the year, for more than three fourths of all General College students listened frequently to such programs. It was interesting to note that of the ten programs most often heard by General College freshmen — Jack Benny (heard by the largest number, 82 per cent), Bing Crosby, the *Hit Parade*, Kay Kyser, Bob Hope, Glenn Miller, Charlie McCarthy, the *Lux Radio Theater*, Elmer Davis, and Fred Waring (heard by 64 per cent) — only two or three might be considered to have a definitely educational purpose. Exactly the same ten programs headed the list reported by students at the end of their sophomore year, evidence of the negligible change that occurred in radio tastes during General College residence. Even the percentage of listeners to each program was almost identical with that discovered for the freshman group. Among news commentators, Paul Sullivan was heard by 30 per cent of the freshmen and by a mere 16 per cent of the sophomores, but a critical news analyst, Raymond Gram Swing, was heard by only 10 per cent of both groups. The *University of Chicago Round Table*, which was listened to by 25 per cent in each group, ranked highest among the programs of a serious and definitely educational nature. Programs of classical music were apparently enjoyed by only 20 to 30 per cent of each group, with the exception of the *Ford Sunday Evening Hour*, which was mentioned by 55 per cent of all the students.

It is rather interesting to note that young people who had been out of the General College for several years had somewhat different tastes in radio programs. This group ranked *Information Please* first and also included the *Ford Sunday Evening Hour*, H. V. Kaltenborn, and *Professor Quiz* among the ten programs they heard most often. These differences in taste suggest that maturation may play as important a role as classroom experiences in determining the selection of radio programs.

Findings obtained from Pace's study of the activities of young adults, many of whom had withdrawn from some division of the university after a year or two of study,[9] were compared with the

[9] Footnote 6, page 106, explains how comparisons were made.

results of the present survey of the activities of former General College students. Analysis of the data on choice of radio programs tended to show that the former General College students had, if anything, somewhat inferior tastes. The vigorous efforts made by the teaching staff to develop discrimination and to give more intelligent direction to students' leisure-time living had apparently not effected much change in actual behavior. Although this was a disquieting discovery, it was probably not very different from what would be found in any college that might seriously seek evidence of the effectiveness of its program in terms of the daily living of its students.

When former students were asked to indicate whether General College courses had stimulated them to any new leisure-time activities or had helped them to improve in any of those in which they had previously engaged, affirmative answers were given by slightly more than one in every four (30 per cent of the graduates and 26 per cent of the nongraduates). No one course was believed by these 253 former students to have contributed particularly to recreational participation, but the first five courses in frequency of mention, with twelve to nineteen endorsements each, were Music Appreciation, Current Affairs, Literature Today, Physical Education, and Art Today. Students' comments given in support of these endorsements reveal some of the ways in which General College courses have probably furthered leisure-time enjoyment.

"Physical Education. Learned some new sports and improved my technique in others."

"Minnesota History gave me a good understanding as to where to go to find places of most interest, historically and otherwise."

"Literature Today. The Writing Laboratory gave me a little more understanding of what contributes to good and bad literature."

"My art course started me with clay modeling, which is now a hobby."

"Took golf in gym. Writing Laboratory helped in literary writing, Art Today in visiting art galleries, Minnesota History in appreciating the *Historic Site Ahead* signs when traveling in Minnesota."

"Art, music, theater, and literature courses have continually kept up my appreciation of all these things, and even though I didn't take photography, seeing what the others did has made me extremely conscious of it as a hobby."

"The gym courses have instilled in me a desire to be a better sportswoman. Current Literature helped me to read more for pleasure. Current Reading gave me an inside view of many magazines that I would not have chosen. All courses helped me in learning to use the library."

"Film and Drama has helped me to enjoy and evaluate movies. Music Today, Art Today, Literature, Film and Drama, Psychology — these subjects gave me much deeper appreciations. My letter writing was improved by the Writing Laboratory."

SUMMARY

The goal of self-understanding set for the General College has been achieved in some measure. In so far as paper-and-pencil tests can give evidence of growth in insights and understandings concerning the nature of human behavior, the data indicate that students enrolled in the General College gain very substantially in these respects during their residence. Furthermore they reveal that courses designed to contribute to these outcomes actually do assist in building the desired understandings.

In the field of attitudes and adjustments, on the other hand, much less growth is apparent, either for the entire student body or for young people enrolled in courses especially designed to promote good personal adjustment. Though there are some distinctly encouraging aspects, such as the gain in social adjustment and the better health attitudes, the most impressive finding is the relative stability in the many traits measured, despite sustained teaching and counseling efforts. It must be remembered, of course, that the tests used in appraising these characteristics were of a paper-and-pencil type and that they leave much to be desired with respect to validity and reliability of measurement. The fact that almost half of all former students acknowledged receiving some help from the General College in dealing with personal and emotional problems also suggests that a more comprehensive evaluation might have revealed contributions not detected by the present tests. All that can be concluded at present is that, according to current methods of assessing personality development, the present curriculum has fallen somewhat short of its hoped-for contributions to this objective.

The free-time activities of General College students or former students are strikingly similar to those of entering students or of young people trained in other programs. Seemingly, out-of-school recreational interests, plans, and activities have not been significantly modified, even by a program organized around the often stressed "human needs." Perhaps even the best program could not do a great deal to offset the influence of tastes developed during the seventeen or eighteen years before students enter college or during the many hours they spend each day in other places than the classroom. But at least much more intensive experimentation is warranted.

CHAPTER 8

Preparation for Home and Family Living

Increasing provisions have been made in the General College program for students to grow in their understanding of problems that touch closely upon their daily living. One area commonly ignored by schools and colleges, that of home and family relationships, has received special attention in the General College because of its importance to students now and in the future. From the very start of the program several euthenics courses have been offered by the university's Division of Home Economics and its School of Business Administration. These dealt with such problems of home and family living as the care of young children, income management, clothing selection, food preparation, and home gardening. In 1938 the General College curriculum was broadened by the introduction of the Home Life Orientation course. This new core course, designed for men as well as women students, provides for the systematic study and discussion of the basic psychology, sociology, and economics of family life today. Likewise the counseling service has given special attention to the difficulties that students may be encountering at home. Thus through many avenues the General College faculty has sought to develop competence on the part of its students in this important area of living.

CHANGES IN KNOWLEDGE OF HOME AND FAMILY LIVING

According to the plan adopted for the other areas, an effort was first made to determine how much students gained in the way of important facts and understandings concerning family life. Tests for this purpose were constructed the summer after the course was first offered (1938–39) and were administered to all students in the fall and again in the spring of the following year. The procedures used in constructing the two forms of this test were the same as those employed in developing the Personal Living Test described in the preceding chapter. The reliability coefficients obtained in the fall for the two forms were .77 (Form A) and .68 (Form B); in the spring the correlation co-efficients were only slightly higher: .79 (Form A) and .72 (Form B). Although the coefficients were not high enough to provide any accurate appraisal of the individual student's knowledge of home and family affairs, the tests still permitted studies of gains made by various groups or classes of students. The following items illustrate the general content of these examinations:

A family that has difficulty in making ends meet should begin economizing by (1) buying only those things for which they can pay cash, (2) selling their car, which is used largely for pleasure and taking the children to school, (3) cutting out all recreations that cost money, (4) keeping careful records of expenditures until they know where the money is going, (5) having the wife do the family laundry, bakery, sewing, and similar work.

Louise, who is three, is very jealous of her little brother, scratching him and tearing at his clothes. It would be wise to (1) put Louise off by herself when she is caught molesting the baby, (2) keep the baby entirely away from Louise, (3) let Louise help in caring for the baby, (4) punish her immediately each time she disturbs the baby, (5) reason with her.

Delinquent children are found more often in neighborhoods in which (1) a large percentage of families own their homes, (2) there are mostly small families, (3) the houses are run down because it isn't worth putting more money into them, (4) the houses are located a long way from the central sections of the city, (5) there are large numbers of foreigners.

John declares that "there is no harm in petting" and that "everyone does it now." His father does not know how to handle the situation. It might be well for the family to (1) warn John that it is immoral and may lead to disastrous consequences, (2) make the question a definite issue on which John's use of the family car and other privileges will depend, (3) punish John severely, (4) encourage John to meet girls and boys at parties where there is little pairing off, (5) forbid John to go out with girls at night.

When the wife works outside the home, the chances for success in family relationships are best if (1) the wife's salary is large, (2) the husband and the wife do similar types of work, (3) the people of the community are not against the idea of married women working, (4) relatives and friends show a great deal of concern and interest in the venture, (5) the wife has hired help in the home.

Scores made on the pretest did not differentiate young people who elected Home Life Orientation during 1939–40 from those who did not elect work in this area, as may be seen in Figure 19.

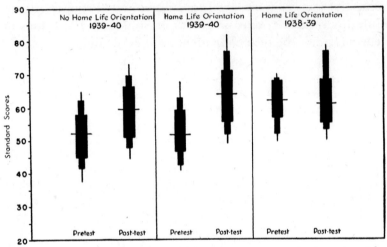

Figure 19. Scores of students who had taken the Home Life Orientation course and those who had not on the Home and Family Relations Test. (See Figures 8 and 14 for explanation.)

Both groups gained so significantly during the year that by the end of the year even the typical student who did not receive special instruction in the problems of home and family living made a score superior to that of more than 75 per cent of the entering freshmen. Students who had taken Home Life Orientation surpassed about 85 per cent of those tested at the beginning of the year.

More precise comparisons of the gains made on this test by those who had been enrolled in the course and those who had not were then undertaken, using covariance techniques that permitted adjustment of the final scores on this test for differences in pretest scores and rank in high school graduating class. The results revealed that students who had taken two or three quarters of Home Life Orientation in 1939–40 gained significantly more than the other students, the F-ratio being 8.15, where a ratio of 6.70 was required to meet the 1 per cent level of significance. Although this gain is statistically significant, it is smaller than the gains made on comparable information tests by students in the other three orientation areas.

Men students made as great an advance in acquiring this type of information as the women did, even though girls are more likely, both in and out of school, to meet the kinds of problems included in the tests.[1] Likewise there was no difference in the gains made during one year by freshmen and sophomores, when their final scores were adjusted for differences in initial performance and in high school rank. Students who had had the course the first year (1938–39) and took the test the next fall not only made scores almost equal to those of students who took the test immediately after they had completed the year's course in Home Life Orientation but also maintained this high level throughout the year. This represents an unusually high degree of retention and suggests either that the information was truly functional, and hence was retained with ease, or that many courses in the college actually implemented what was taught in Home Life Orientation.

CHANGES IN ATTITUDES

Two of the measures included in the regular testing program — the Minnesota Personality Scale and the Bell Adjustment Inventory — contain sections relating to family adjustment. As was indicated in Chapter 7, General College entrants could not be differentiated from students in the College of Science, Literature, and the Arts by means of the scores they made on the family adjustment section of the Minnesota Scale, for General College men ranked at the forty-seventh percentile and General College women at the forty-eighth percentile of the distribution of scores made by freshmen in the College of Science, Literature, and the Arts. The fact that almost exactly the same scores were

[1] In this particular year (1939–40) women outnumbered men by a three to one ratio in the Home Life Orientation course.

made by General College students at the end of the year, suggests that in so far as favorable family adjustment is revealed by scores on this test no measurable improvement occurred during a year of General College residence.[2] Exactly the same conclusions were reached after an analysis of the beginning and end-of-the-year scores on the Family Adjustment section of the Bell Inventory. Since the average score made by men students remained unchanged, they continued to show average (as defined by Bell) adjustment to these problems. The gain in average scores for women students, which resulted in an advance from the *average* to the *good* category, was not sufficiently large to be statistically significant, even at the 5 per cent level.

Pre- and post-test scores on these sections of the Bell Inventory and the Minnesota Personality Scale were studied by analysis of variance techniques to find out whether students who took work in Home Life Orientation were differentiated from other General College students in their attitudes toward family problems, at either the beginning or the end of the year. These analyses were made separately for men and women, since it is conceivable that the sexes might be affected differently by such a course. Yet not a single significant difference, even at the 5 per cent level, was discovered in eight comparisons between instructed and uninstructed students. It seems safe to conclude, therefore, that this course had not significantly improved family adjustment, as this is measured by the Bell Inventory and the Minnesota Scale. Opinions of former students given in a later section of this chapter suggest that discussion of these problems actually did exert some influences not assayed by these tests.

In order to find out what students thought about a good many issues and problems in family living, a questionnaire covering some of these points was formulated by the two instructors in Home Life Orientation. This inventory contained two hundred items, thus affording students an extended opportunity to express their present opinions concerning relationships with their parents, their brothers and sisters, members of the other sex, and

[2] See Figures 15, 16, and 17 in the preceding chapter.

their future husbands or wives as well as issues involved in the personal management of money, family budgeting, women working outside the home, and divorce.

Illustrative are these items. By encircling one of three indicators — *yes, no,* or *?* — following each item, the student expressed his considered opinion.

A man should have the major responsibility for earning the family income and the woman for spending it.

If a careful plan for spending does not work, the family may assume that it is one of the families that cannot run on a definite budget.

Children below high school age should not be expected to help with the work at home.

Parents should accept, without interference, the friendships of their children after they reach high school age.

Legislation should be passed making it impossible for a married woman to hold a job if her husband is employed.

Only married people or those about to be married should be given information about birth control.

One evidence of successful family life is that the young people of the family would rather be at home than anywhere else.

Other items answered by encircling one position on a clearly defined five-point scale were these:

Parents fuss too much about the things their sons and daughters do.

The youngest children are likely to be spoiled.

Family ties are strengthened when times get tough.

Marriages are a result of convenience or of the proximity of the couple who plan to marry.

Parents are wet blankets.

This questionnaire was administered at the beginning of the year to practically all freshmen, but so many examinations were included in the final battery given the following May that it was readministered only to the students enrolled in Home Life Orientation. This drastically reduced the number of cases available for study, since only forty-four students had filled out both questionnaires. As indicated by the results given in Table 5, differences significant at the 1 per cent level were obtained for only fourteen items out of the two hundred included in this questionnaire. The most marked changes occurred on items concerning

TABLE 5. ITEMS SHOWING SIGNIFICANT DIFFERENCES IN THE ATTITUDES OF STUDENTS TAKING THE HOME LIFE ORIENTATION COURSE

Items	Percentages Giving Yes Response		
	Post-test	Pre-test	CR
The father and mother should work out the budget alone when children are below high school age.....	89	39	6.0
Children should be sheltered from unpleasant experiences	55	16	4.5
Both boys and girls should obey their parents without question as long as they are being supported by them	66	25	4.5
It is all right for a married woman to work if she doesn't have enough to do at home................	20	55	3.8
Children at every age level should be required to account for the way they spend money their parents give them...	48	16	3.7
All members of the family, except infants, should determine how the family income should be spent.....	30	61	3.4
Divorce should be granted on grounds of adultery...	80	98	3.2
It is possible for a young person to be too attached to his parents	66	91	3.0
Outside agencies are taking an increasing interest in family welfare	68	91	3.0
It is all right for a married woman to work if earnings are necessary for a comfortable standard of living..	84	100	3.0
Parents should make the final decision as to the movies children under fourteen years of age attend........	86	64	2.8
A young person, planning to marry, should keep in mind that he is marrying the individual and not the whole family	87	68	2.8
The religious beliefs of the family definitely influence family relationships	55	80	2.8
The mother in the home should have full responsibility for the care of the home........................	77	52	2.8

parent-child relationships. For example, at the end of the year students were far less ready to assent to entire control of budget-making by the parents when the children are under high school age, to strict obedience to parents in the whole period during which children are supported, or to a sheltering of children from unpleasant experiences. On only eight items, in addition to the fourteen given in the table, were differences discovered to be significant at the 5 per cent level, so that on 177 items there was practically no alteration during the year. Because of the limited number of cases available, few generalizations can be drawn from the present results. They do suggest, however, that not a great deal of influence was exerted in this direction either by the Home Life Orientation course or by all the other experiences to which young people were exposed during the year.

HOME-LIFE ACTIVITIES OF FORMER STUDENTS

When young people who had been out of the General College for several years were asked many of the same questions that had been included in Pace's study, about their present interests, activities, and needs in the area of home and family living, they gave answers surprisingly like those supplied by young adults who had had no contact with a general education program.[3] For example, among twenty-five problems canvassed, the nine items yielding differences above the 5 per cent level indicated that the young people surveyed in the adult study were more interested than were General College students in gaining information on such problems as whether one should rent, buy, or build a home, what constitutes proper humidity, how much money should be spent for food, how one should meet a child's emotional problems, and what one's legal rights and obligations are as a renter or home owner. It must be remembered, of course, that these former General College students had not had the new Home Life Orientation course, though many of them had taken euthenics courses covering some of the same materials. Whether these results were obtained because General College students already knew the answers to these questions or because they really had little genuine interest in such problems cannot be determined from the present data.

Among the various listed activities only three in this area yielded significant differences, which indicated that former General College students were more likely to hunt food bargains, plan budgets, and buy phonograph records than were students from other colleges (see Table 6). Also the non-General College students did a little more rearranging of furniture. Except on

[3] Pace, *They Went to College*, pp. 79–91. See also page 106, footnote 6, for an explanation of how comparisons were made.

TABLE 6. OUT-OF-SCHOOL ACTIVITIES AND INTERESTS OF FORMER STUDENTS MOST CLEARLY DIFFERENTIATING THOSE WHO ATTENDED THE GENERAL COLLEGE FROM THOSE WHO ATTENDED OTHER COLLEGES IN THE UNIVERSITY *

Greater Participation or Interest Shown by Former General College Students (Differences significant at least at the 5 per cent level)	Greater Participation or Interest Shown by Other Former Students (Differences significant at least at the 5 per cent level)
1. Wrote reports as part of job	1. Planned work for others to do
2. Interviewed clients or customers	2. Bought new mechanical equipment
3. Prepared or signed legal papers	3. Prepared charts or graphs
4. Paid dues for hospitalization	4. Studied new mechanical processes in production
5. Planned definite medical and dental care	5. Recognized many advantages of present job
6. Took regular physical exercise	6. Rearranged furniture for comfort and convenience
7. Planned expenditures on a budget basis	7. Wanted to know more about food purchasing, child care, home maintenance
8. Hunted for clothing bargains	
9. Bought phonograph records	8. Desired more information about health problems
10. Engaged in individual sports	9. Listened extensively to radio programs
11. Went to picnics	10. Read many books and magazines for pleasure
12. Attended concerts	
13. Discussed propaganda control and armaments	11. Engaged in general conversation
14. Listened to presidential broadcasts	12. Played cards
15. Wanted to know more about health dangers, income taxes, foreign developments	13. Expressed more leisure-time preferences: drama, reading, traveling, art
	14. Voted in public elections
	15. Discussed public relief, New Deal, public debt, capital-labor fight

* The table summarizes all differences discovered between General and non-General College students. Therefore it includes many activities relating to personal, vocational, or socio-civic areas rather than home or family living.

these four items it was impossible to differentiate between the two groups with respect to out-of-school activities.

ATTITUDES OF FORMER STUDENTS TOWARD THEIR COURSES IN HOME AND FAMILY LIVING

In the questionnaire sent to former students one question read, "Have any General College courses assisted you in meeting problems of family relationship or management (arising in your own home, if you are married, or in the home of which you are now a member, if you are unmarried)? If so, what courses? And how have they helped?" The majority of students gave negative answers; 33 per cent of those who received the A.A. degree and 22 per cent of those who had dropped out acknowledged assistance in this area. The relatively small proportion of students who believed that they had received help on such problems is in part due to the less frequent election of courses in this area than in several others. Whatever the cause, however, the fact remains that former students are not as aware of the influence of the General College program on this phase of their living as on several other frontiers.

The four courses specified as being most helpful were Psychology, which ranked first by a decisive margin, Human Biology, Human Development, and Euthenics. These evaluations were made, of course, by students who had left college before the new Home Life Orientation course was introduced. Some of the comments supporting affirmative responses are as follows:

"Psychology has helped me to get along better with people."

"I married a General College girl, and we are just as happy as if we were a couple of Phi Betes."

"Euthenics has given me a better understanding of purchasing clothing and furniture for my home, especially as to quality."

"The course in Human Biology helped because there are welfare children in my home, some of whom are borderline cases of feeble-mindedness. This course helps one to understand these people better and how to treat them."

"Human Development and Personal Adjustment, Euthenics, Practical Applications of Psychology, Straight and Crooked Thinking — I believe these courses have helped me to understand my family better and have helped me in taking care of my own chores in the home."

"Human Development, Psychology, Philosophy — these courses, especially, answered my questions and actually made it possible for me to meet problems and make decisions accordingly. I can't begin to write in such a small space of all the ways — in my attitude toward my family, in my everyday life, and in my plans for the future — that the above courses have helped me."

"Psychology, Human Biology, and Individual Family Resources have helped me to understand why members of my family do and say certain things. I check myself sometimes when I become nervous or overexcited. Every now and then I am able to help my family or myself in some little way by something I learned in Human Biology."

SUMMARY

Studies of the extent to which students, during their General College residence, augmented their understanding of home and family problems and made more effective adjustments to them have resulted in findings similar to those set forth in the preceding chapter, dealing with students' growth in self-understanding and social skills.

In general, students gain significantly in their knowledge of the psychology, sociology, and economics of family living. In these types of understanding the largest gains were made by those young people who were enrolled in the core course, Home Life Orientation. Though the gains that could be specifically attributed to instruction were perhaps not quite as striking as might have been hoped, they nevertheless showed that courses specifically established for a given purpose actually do assist students in attaining the desired goal. Moreover, since these analyses revealed that the students retained the knowledge they had gained at least a year after instruction ended, it appears to have become a well-organized part of their background.

In the area of attitudes and adjustments, on the other hand, there was only a slight suggestion, derived from the most fallible of the three indicators used, that either residence in the General College or specific instruction given in the Home Life Orientation course brought about any real changes. The major finding that emerged from these analyses was that family adjustment, as it is being currently measured, was not noticeably affected by this particular program of general education. With this finding most former students seemed to agree, since less than a third believed that General College courses had enabled them to solve more effectively their problems of family relationship or management. This does not mean, of course, that discussions of home and family problems had not been of benefit to them, nor does it indicate what the new Home Life Orientation course may now be accomplishing. The findings simply suggest that more careful study be given to the question of what actual changes are wrought in students' thinking and living by systematic instruction concerning home and family problems.

CHAPTER 9

Vocational Readiness

Since eight out of ten General College students do not continue in college beyond their sophomore year, the preparation that they have received for earning a living becomes one searching and thoroughly practical test of the value of their schooling. That General College students stand in special need of vocational help is evidenced in many ways, as, for example, by the obviously misguided choices of careers that many of them express at entrance to college. In these unrealistic aims they are abetted by their parents, whose thinking is dominated by middle-class attitudes toward vocational problems. As Williams has pointed out, "Having usually achieved some measure of security without benefit of higher education, fathers expect their sons and daughters to attain marked financial, economic, and vocational successes because of the greater benefits of a university education. . . . Interviews with parents on their ambitions for their children revealed a strong belief in the inherent goodness and the prestige value of a higher education and an uncritical and unrealistic belief that the mere possession of a college degree would be an open sesame to all the finer things in life." [1] Because of these facts the General College staff has felt especially obligated to present realistically the values that accrue from attending college and by every means available to guide students toward vocational opportunities suited to their individual and special needs. Reference to the statement of objectives given in Chapter 3 will show how thoroughly this was the concern of the whole faculty.

Courses dealing with vocational information and the techniques of making valid job choices have been offered since the

[1] *Curriculum-Making in the General College*, pp. 63, 71.

opening of the college in 1932. In 1938 vocational orientation became one of the four core areas introduced into the curriculum. The course in Vocational Orientation was not designed to take the place of individual vocational counseling, which continued to be available to all students. As it actually worked out, however, a substantial minority did not seek advisement on vocational problems, so that it became possible to compare the effectiveness of the course implemented by counseling with that of the course alone. Because of the obvious importance both to the students and the staff of the university this area was selected for intensive study by the University of Minnesota Committee on Educational Research. The results of the study, which was sponsored by a special committee and directed by C. Harold Stone, will be quoted freely in certain sections of this chapter.

STUDENTS' UNDERSTANDING OF VOCATIONAL TRENDS AND PROBLEMS

The intelligent choice of a career presumably rests on adequate information concerning the requirements of various sorts of jobs, personal qualifications for these jobs — abilities, background, and interests — and vocational opportunities available in a particular community or regional area. How much knowledge of this type is gained by students in the General College was therefore critically investigated. As in similar surveys of the other orientation areas, a broad-gauged examination was constructed through the cooperative efforts of the instructional staff for the area and the evaluators. The process was greatly simplified by the existence of a large file of validated test items accumulated during the years when Choice of an Occupation had been offered as an elective course and also by the willingness of the entire General College faculty to serve as critics.

As in the case of the tests for the other areas, the new test was prepared in two forms, each requiring forty-five minutes for administration.[2] It was given to every student in the General College in the fall of 1939 and again in the spring of 1940.[3] The

[2] Chapter 7, pp. 95–117.
[3] Covariance analyses indicated no differences, even at the 5 per cent level of significance, that could be attributed to the particular combination of tests used (AA, AB, BA, and BB).

reliability coefficients for the fall testing were .81 (Form A) and .85 (Form B); for the spring testing, .85 for both forms. Illustrative items are as follows:

In the *Help Wanted — Men* section of city papers, the largest number of jobs are offered for (1) clerks, (2) restaurant workers, (3) salesmen, (4) mechanics, (5) tradesmen.

The largest number of fatal accidents occur (1) in the home, (2) in automobiles, (3) on trains, (4) in airplanes, (5) at work.

Selling demands many qualities. The most important single quality in the list below is (1) abstract intelligence, (2) social intelligence, (3) clerical ability, (4) executive ability, (5) ability in mental arithmetic.

To obtain the most reliable information about one's aptitudes and abilities, it is best to consult (1) a teacher in occupations, (2) a trained vocational counselor, (3) an astrologer, (4) a psychiatrist, (5) a college program adviser.

The amount of training required of a master workman varies according to the particular trade. The greatest amount of training would be needed to become a (1) carpenter, (2) bricklayer, (3) radio repairman, (4) auto mechanic, (5) cabinetmaker.

Many very different kinds of work are related through the ability that is needed to perform the work. The painter of miniatures and the surgeon both need (1) social intelligence, (2) mathematical ability, (3) clerical ability, (4) fine eye-hand coordination, (5) artistic ability.

As Figure 20 shows, most young people who remain in the college for at least one year increase their understanding of the vocational problems and issues that are measured by the present test. This happens whether or not they enroll in a course specifically designed to promote this type of knowledge. For example, the gain made by the typical General College freshman who had not taken Vocational Orientation was of such magnitude that by the end of the year his performance exceeded that achieved by more than 65 per cent of all entering freshmen. The spring scores for these students compared favorably with the beginning-of-the-year scores made by a representative group of students in the College of Science, Literature, and the Arts, despite the large differences between the academic abilities and backgrounds of the two groups.

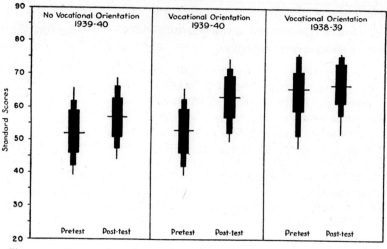

Figure 20. Scores of students who had taken the Vocational Orientation course and those who had not on the Vocational Orientation Test. (See Figures 8 and 14 for explanation.)

Young people who had been enrolled in Vocational Orientation made much greater strides than other students in acquiring these types of information. Thus by the end of the year the typical student who had taken at least two quarters' work in this field surpassed almost 85 per cent of the entering freshman class. Analyses of covariance made much clearer the decisive nature of this gain, for when corrections were applied for initial inequalities in high school rank and scores on the pretest it became clear that students in Vocational Orientation had made far more progress than other students. The F-ratio, for example, was 20.89, whereas the 1 per cent level of significance would require a ratio of only 3.83. Even more impressive was the gain made by young people who not only took the core course but also tried the comprehensive examination given only to students who presented fifteen hours' work in the vocational orientation area. In this instance the F-ratio rose to 24.20, far above the 1 per cent level of significance (3.83).

Students who had taken Vocational Orientation the preceding year made scores on the fall tests that closely approximated the end-of-the-year performance of trained freshmen, as may be seen in Figure 20. In other words, the tests seemingly probed insights and understandings sufficiently organized and meaningful to be retained several months after formal instruction in the area was completed. The high level of the scores made by these same students in the spring of their sophomore year showed only a slight loss in these types of information and suggested that other courses and the counseling service might have implemented the experiences gained in the Vocational Orientation course.

Other studies of these test results revealed no appreciable difference in the amount of gain made by men and women students in information about vocational trends and needs. Similar covariance analyses indicated that freshmen and sophomores were not differentiated in the extent of this gain. These facts would seem to indicate that the Vocational Orientation course and the other offerings of the General College that were designed to promote an understanding of vocational problems had about equal value for these various groups.

Taken as a whole, the present data revealed that instruction definitely made a difference in students' understanding of vocational problems. While uninstructed students also gained in these types of information, special courses have provided the sound factual background and the broad insight necessary for the proper selection of a career and of the training appropriate to it.

CHANGES IN VOCATIONAL ATTITUDES

The character of the vocational goals that young people set for themselves, the wages they expect, and their hopes and plans for securing suitable preparation also supply relevant information for the appraisal of the General College vocational program.

As Stone has shown, General College young people were only slightly less optimistic at the end of a year or two of residence than they had been in the beginning when they were asked about the salaries they hoped to receive when they had completed their first year on a job, when they had completed five years, and when they had reached their peak of efficiency.[4] Al-

[4] C. Harold Stone, "Evaluation Program in Vocational Orientation," in *Studies in Higher Education,* Biennial Report of the Committee on Educational Research, 1938–40, pp. 130–45.

though students enrolled in the Vocational Orientation course had learned about the limited number of professional, semiprofessional, and managerial positions and about the intense competition to which young people are subjected in aspiring to such jobs, they still expected to receive the same salaries as did students in the uninstructed groups. At the end of this year of special instruction, for example, the men expected to earn approximately $120 a month during their first year on the job, $250 a month after five years of work, and $450 a month at their peak. The estimates given by the women were more conservative — approximately $85 a month for the first year, $140 at the end of five years, and $190 at their highest point.

Some changes did occur, however, in the attitudes of students toward different types of jobs. Evidence on this point was obtained from students' selection of three out of eight suggested areas, in which they believed their talents might find the most appropriate expression. By the close of the freshman year the group as a whole was significantly less favorable toward occupations that usually require rather extended preparation, such as social service and artistic, technical, or scientific types of work. Yet the Vocational Orientation course was apparently not responsible for this change, since it was just as evident among General College students not enrolled in it. None of the groups showed significant changes in attitude toward occupations involving business contacts and business detail, which ranked high at the beginning and the end of the year.

Changes in actual job choices, however, pointed toward a greater realism on the part of students enrolled in the Vocational Orientation course. Whereas the uninstructed students had tended to become more ambitious in their vocational aims, departing even further from the occupational classifications of their fathers, the choices of trained students were less ambitious, particularly with respect to jobs at the professional level. At the end of the year only half as many of these students as at the beginning aspired to be engineers, lawyers, teachers, or doctors.

On both occasions when students listed their vocational choices they also specified how certain they were that they would actually be able to follow these careers. When responses given by the same students at the beginning and the end of the year were compared, it was clear that they had tended to become somewhat less certain — undoubtedly a wholesome outcome in view of the fantastic and clearly illogical goals originally expressed by many of them. Nevertheless there was only slight evidence that students enrolled in the Vocational Orientation course became more critical of their vocational plans than students without this special training. The small changes that occurred may therefore have been due more largely to individual counseling than to formal instruction in the Vocational Orientation course.

REASONABLENESS OF VOCATIONAL CHOICE

The experiences provided by the General College in the vocational Orientation area had been chosen particularly to assist students in selecting the right types of jobs. The next step was to find out whether the changes that did occur in vocational choices were in a direction more in accord with the students' own patterns of interests, abilities, and capacities. Stone therefore arranged for a rating of the suitability of each student's choice by members of the General College counseling staff from data provided by the extensive test and interview reports found in his individual case folder.[5] In this rating four classifications were used — *Optimal* for cases in which the student's choice coincided with both the field and level of job suggested by the counselor, *Fair* for those in which the student's choice was in the same field but at a different level from the counselor's rating, or in which the level seemed appropriate but the field differed, *Poor* for those in which neither field nor level coincided, and *No choice* for those in which the student had made no vocational decision. When these ratings, based on choices expressed by students at the beginning and again at the end of the year, were compared, the percentage of poor choices was not reduced in either the group that had received special instruction in voca-

[5] Stone, "Evaluation Program in Vocational Orientation," pp. 139–40. Definitions of the job levels and fields of activity employed in making these ratings are given in the Stone study.

tional orientation or in the control, or uninstructed, group. The findings showed clearly that individual counseling was a more important factor than course instruction in improving vocational choices, but that students who received both counseling and instruction in vocational orientation made the most marked gains To quote from Stone's report:

"When no consideration was given to the counseling received by students, the percentage of poor choices was not reduced and the increase in proportion of optimal choices was insignificant. However, when the students who received vocational counseling during the year were separated from those who were not counseled, some rather marked differences were discovered. . . . The counseled students have a higher proportion of optimal choices at the end of the year and those not counseled have a smaller proportion of optimal choices. . . . *Students who received instruction in vocational orientation in addition to individual counseling* made very marked gains in the proportion of optimal choices by the end of the year." [6]

VOCATIONAL ACTIVITIES AND ATTITUDES OF FORMER STUDENTS

Knowledge of the jobs in which former General College students are now engaged should assist materially in appraising the program, as well as in determining the responsibilities of the college toward future groups of students. Therefore young people who had recently withdrawn from the General College were studied to find out what types of jobs they had and what plans they had for further training.

Sales work predominated among the jobs held by those who had been out of school only one or two years; next in order were clerical work and the semiskilled trades. The very brief descriptions of these positions, which often included nothing beyond the job title, precluded any classification of jobs on the basis of the amount of special training they required. The general impression obtained from studying lists of these jobs, however, is that few former students took positions that required specialized skills or understandings. A great many appear to have taken

[6] *Ibid.*, p. 140.

whatever jobs they could commandeer, as did a host of other young people — trained or untrained. About 10 per cent of the boys and 35 per cent of the girls who had recently left school reported neither jobs nor further schooling and thus indicated that quite a number of young people face unemployment in their first year or two out of college. About 10 per cent of the employed young people held only part-time jobs.

About 15 per cent of these young persons appeared to be taking any sort of training, either on a part-time or on an extension basis, that might lead to job advancement. It seems unlikely, therefore, that the high vocational goals set by many General College freshmen will be attained. For the most part these young people seem destined to join the ranks of undistinguished, hard-working middle-class adults.

Likewise those out of school for several years have moved up only a few rungs on the vocational ladder. For example, whereas 50 per cent of the entering freshmen selected vocational goals that would be classified in the two highest categories of the Minnesota Occupational Scale, less than 6 per cent of those who had recently dropped out held such jobs, and only 12 per cent of those out of school from three to seven years now had such jobs or appeared to be working toward them.

In their job activities and interests students who had received the Associate in Arts degree could seldom be distinguished from those who had left the General College before graduation. When these former students were asked to check the activities that their jobs involved, the only difference that met even the 5 per cent level of significance was the preparation of more charts or graphs by the nongraduate group. In measured job satisfaction [7] the two groups were almost identical. In other words, those who had completed their general education program gave no more evidence of being happy in their present positions than did other students. Similarly among fifteen suggested problems in this vocational area, the only evidence of any real difference in atti-

---

[7] An abbreviated form of the Hoppock Scale of Job Satisfaction had been included in the Pace questionnaire by permission of the author and was reproduced in the 16-page blank used with former General College students.

tude between nongraduates and graduates occurred on an item about where to obtain training for advancement. More graduates than nongraduates were interested in acquiring such information. The fact that only occasional differences were found in the job activities and attitudes of those who had received degrees and those who had dropped out is probably not surprising, since the program was not designed to provide vocational training.

Queried concerning the possible vocational values of General College courses, only a minority stated, in varying degrees of enthusiasm and certainty, that the curriculum had been of real assistance. For example, only one student in four (27 per cent) answered affirmatively to the question "Did your General College training help you to secure your first job?" Another 3 per cent were undecided, and the rest gave definitely negative responses. The comments that supported these judgments were rather revealing. Among students who attributed vocational values to the General College curriculum, the following remarks are typical:

"I feel that my having had two years of college training influenced my first employer to select me from a number of applicants."

"Gave a broad scope of knowledge. Helped me to talk to prospective employers with confidence."

"My rating in the vocational guidance examination gave me confidence that I couldn't have obtained elsewhere."

"My General College courses did more than any others to give me a well-rounded education."

"The course in Business Mathematics got me interested in actuarial work."

"Gave me self-confidence and poise in approaching prospective employers. Gave me tact to meet customers and handle business arrangements. Gave me precision and thoroughness in detail work."

Former students who did not find their General College work particularly helpful expressed the following attitudes:

"Our company does not require college education. A high school graduate with an average amount of intelligence is preferred because he can be trained before his ideas are too well set."

"My work is of a technical nature, and therefore my General College training did not directly help me in securing my job."

"Can't say it did, though it may have had something to do with it. It was almost two years later that I found employment."

"This college might have enlarged my general knowledge, but if so I could not notice this. Law school was decisive."

"No. I did not take any subject which has helped me."

"Not at all, since I didn't specialize in any field. The only thing I was eligible for was clerking, which is really suited to any high school graduate."

When asked whether their General College training had helped them to hold their jobs or to gain advancement, only a fourth of the group (26 per cent) gave an affirmative answer. Illustrative of their replies are the following:

"I gained a fairly wide knowledge on many subjects, which naturally helped in my advancement."

"Naturally any position requires studying and continued learning. The General College taught me how to study in order to gain advancement."

"The self-confidence which I acquired aided me in . . . meeting the public efficiently. It also spurred me to ask for raises and advancements, which I got."

"It gave me a certain prestige that this store really requires."

The much larger numbers (59 per cent) who felt that their General College study had contributed little to job advancement expressed such opinions as these:

"My job was selling. I didn't learn to sell in the General College."

"The college training is theory. My job is practical."

"My abilities and willingness to work, and my personality, were the reasons for my advancement in this work."

"I didn't take any subjects in the General College that have as yet tied into anything I have worked at."

"This is what is frequently referred to as a 'blind-alley job.' There is no advancement to get to it and no advancement from it."

In answer to still another query, "Have any General College courses helped you in earning a living?" more than a fourth of the group (28 per cent) described vocational values obtained from at least one course. As one would obviously expect from the nature of the General College curriculum, the positive outcomes stressed by students are found rather in increased general understanding and better personal adjustment than in specialized

OUTCOMES OF GENERAL EDUCATION

or technical preparation for the job. This is well illustrated in the following comments that accompanied affirmative answers.

"Psychology and Sociology, in dealing with people in the right way."

"How to Study (efficiency), Vocations (scientific approach), Current Affairs and Formation of Public Opinion (intellectual interests broadened), these are all indirect, though important in teaching."

"If any General College course has helped me it was Textiles. I learned certain technical phrases which made people think I knew what I was talking about."

"Courses in Public Opinion and Psychology. In meeting people of all nationalities, races, and creeds, when delivering beer, one must know when, where, how, and what to talk about."

"Writing Laboratory helped a great deal in writing business letters. Psychology helped in meeting customers, handling other employees, etc."

"Business Mathematics and Psychology. They helped in working with figures in an office and in handling customers and other clerks while working on the floor."

Most of the students who gave negative answers to this question added no supporting comment. The few who added some explanation to their *No response* sometimes revealed by their answers that they had obtained some help, though it had not been along the line of direct job preparation. Thus the following comments were made:

"With reservations. The general knowledge may have been helpful, but no specific course has aided me."

"They haven't helped me in making a living, but have in other ways."

"I have used none of the knowledge I gained in General College."

Almost half of these former students indicated that they had had helpful talks with General College faculty members or counselors concerning their vocational plans, many giving impressive evidence of the values of this service. On the other hand, a few of the replies made by those who said that these talks were helpful could hardly be classed as enthusiastic testimonies. The following comments are representative of those accompanying *Yes* replies:

"They helped me when I got discouraged and built up my morale when it was low."

"At the time I had a talk with one of the faculty members, it was very discouraging to me. I was to have a very sad future, according to him. He considered only academic marks and such trivialities that really mean little when out making a living, selling in particular."

"My talks with ———— were of definite value. . . . They gave me new confidence and increased my desire for vocational training."

"I was convinced by this faculty that I should change schools and in so doing I completely changed the entire course of my life. It improved me a great deal."

"I had a very enlightening conversation with a counselor concerning my studying to be a psychologist. I was told I had a better chance to become a mail carrier."

"Helped find out what I was *not* fitted for but not what I was fitted for."

"I had full knowledge of my inclinations and abilities and knew what to seek when looking for work, or in managing my married life, because of advice of counselors."

Former students who reported little personal value from the counseling service acknowledged that in many cases they had not taken advantage of it or had not tried to follow out the plans recommended to them.

"I believe that this is for the most part my own fault. If there were any such opportunities, I did not avail myself of them."

"A consultation wasn't necessary because I had definite vocational plans before entering the General College."

"I never felt that my vocational plans were correctly analyzed at the time, and as a result all conferences were unsatisfactory."

"I remember somebody over there suggested I get out and do manual labor, and I'd like to inform that guy there isn't a callous on my hands yet. I admit I was never a student."

"I continued in the exact opposite. So the advice given, though good, served only as a temporary bar. I should have known better."

General College graduates were also compared in their job activities and attitudes with young people who had dropped out of other colleges, since these two groups are closely comparable in ability.[8] In the activities engaged in on the job a few rather

[8] Pace, *They Went to College*, pp. 92–108. See also page 106, footnote 6, for an explanation of how comparisons were made.

definite differences appeared. General College graduates engaged more frequently in such activities as interviewing clients or customers, writing reports, and preparing or signing contracts or legal papers. The non-General College students participated more often in such activities as studying new mechanical processes for producing goods, selecting new mechanical equipment, preparing charts or graphs, dictating letters or reports, and planning work for others to do.

Though no differences appeared between these two groups on the Hoppock Scale of Job Satisfaction, the non-General College students indicated, by their responses in another section of the blank, that they found many more advantages in their present jobs than the General College group did. For example, eight of the fourteen differences exceeded the 1 per cent level of significance and these all showed a deeper conviction on the part of the non-General College group that they were earning good salaries, enjoying steady employment, being advanced on the basis of merit, having contacts with many pleasant people, being afforded opportunities for initiative, being granted reasonable freedom on the job, doing work in line with their abilities, and being given proper recognition for the work they did.

The two groups did not differ significantly in the extent to which they felt need for further training. Likewise, among all groups of former students the goals they set for the future were largely self-centered, focused on the desire for personal, family, and job security and happiness. Highly disquieting, too, was the fact that in no group did a majority of the men or of the women feel that it was especially important to keep informed about social changes and other matters that might affect their health and their safety on the job. As much as 40 per cent of the two groups did not feel any special need to know more about economic trends or changes in government that would unquestionably affect their jobs.

SUMMARY

This survey can only confirm the judgment of these young people that their problem is basically an economic one. All students clearly need more realistic discussions of the specific requirements of jobs, of personal abilities and disabilities in relation to these requirements, and of actual employment possibilities in their own communities. Furthermore many evidences point toward the necessity for more actual training in college for the jobs that students must some day hold.

To some of these ends the General College program has definitely contributed. For example, young people enrolled in courses specifically organized for vocational orientation gained significantly in their understanding of job requirements and of the nature of the human abilities needed for various kinds of work. Students not enrolled in the Vocational Orientation course also gained some of this knowledge, though not as much.

Changes in attitudes were less impressive. Though some students changed their minds about the kinds of jobs they preferred, they did not alter the salary expectations that they held when they entered college. Only those young people who had received individual counseling were able to make more appropriate choices of careers. For students without counseling, even for those enrolled in special vocational courses, the proportion of optimal vocational choices did not increase, nor did the proportion of poor choices decrease during a year in the General College. The situation has its hopeful aspects, however, for when young people did take advantage of the many existent resources for vocational orientation or reorientation — the special vocational courses and the individualized assistance of trained counselors — marked changes did occur in their ambitions. The fact that some young people seemed to be so little influenced may be due perhaps not so much to faulty features in the program itself as to the absence of effective contact on the part of many students with its available services.

CHAPTER 10

Socio-Civic Competence

A conviction that college should effectually prepare young people for the responsibilities and privileges of citizenship, both now and in their long out-of-school years, has undergirded the General College venture from its very start. During the earliest years of the program, more than half of all the courses offered were aimed at deepening students' understanding of the social, economic, and political order and inclining their thinking toward socially worth-while goals. One evidence of this interest was the requirement that each student take a comprehensive examination attesting his acquaintance with current affairs. In more recent years the social studies courses have been reorganized; a new core area in socio-civic orientation has been established to provide for a broader orientation of young people to the life of the community, state, and nation. One of the comprehensive subject-matter areas, that of the social science studies, designed for students who have passed the socio-civic comprehensive examination, has permitted more intensive study of these same problems. In addition, socio-civic courses have been used generously in fulfilling requirements for comprehensive examinations in other areas. As a result, approximately two fifths of all the course work now taken by General College students deals with problems of history, government, economics, and sociology.

Because of this unusually heavy curricular emphasis on the social studies, as well as the intrinsic value of the materials presented, it is no wonder that many of the objectives of the General College were clearly directed toward the development of socio-civic competence. Hence in evaluating the program it becomes important to inquire into the changes that occur in General College students' knowledge and understanding of social problems, in their points of view toward these problems, and in their actual participation in the life of their own campus and community. Because an effort has been made in this evaluation to examine many different kinds of changes, it has been impossible to study in much detail the special contributions of particular courses. Though some exploratory studies of this latter type have been made, the present results on the whole simply suggest the ways in which this general education program has influenced its students. Later studies of the same data should permit identification of the particular courses that are most and least productive of desired types of growth.

GAINS IN SOCIAL, CIVIC, AND ECONOMIC INFORMATION

Several tests were used to appraise the students' knowledge and understanding of basic social concepts, of historical events that have a direct bearing on present-day life, of economic and social trends, and of current public affairs. Since these tests sampled important facts and relationships more broadly than do the usual course examinations, they gave the students ample opportunity to show what they had gained from independent reading, radio listening, and observation of life in the community, as well as from regular classroom instruction. Although all the understandings that were tested may not be demonstrably pertinent to the building of social competence, they furnish a background for critical thinking about social action. Young people who know little about the social order of which they are a part can scarcely be expected to enter intelligently into the varied civic responsibilities that await them.

As one means of studying gains in information or understanding, a test was constructed to sample certain outcomes deemed important by those teaching in the socio-civic area. Since the present study began in the fall of 1938, at the same time that the two new core courses were first offered, a socio-civic affairs test was formulated during that year and administered as a pre- and post-test to all General College students the following year. While this procedure necessarily limited any study of gains to a single year, the use of both freshman and sophomore groups resulted in a reasonably accurate estimate of how much growth occurred in these types of understanding during the entire two-year period.

The new Socio-Civic Affairs Test was developed by the co-operative procedure described elsewhere, the instructors supplying most of the actual content and the evaluation staff assisting in phrasing and editing the test items.[1] Two forms were prepared, with the items balanced as well as could be done from inspection of the items and from results of item analyses of earlier examinations. Illustrative items are as follows:

If a business is said to be "open shop" this means that (1) its employees belong to a union, (2) it will not permit any of its employees to belong to a union, (3) workers do not have to belong to a union in order to hold their jobs, (4) it encourages its employees to form a "company union," (5) it is open for full inspection by government officials.

One of the best ways to judge a presidential candidate's social and economic beliefs is to consider (1) his campaign speeches, (2) the political party under whose name he is running, (3) the national platform of his political party, (4) the kinds of individuals and groups who support him, (5) his religious affiliation.

Inevitable aftermath of all wars is (1) defeat of democracy, (2) economic depression, (3) rise of Communism, (4) marked increase in employment, (5) organization of an international governing body.

Many significant developments have taken place in Minnesota during the last 20 years. Some of the changes listed below are true and some are false. In the space at the left of each item write a plus (+) to indicate each change or development that has occurred, and write a zero (0) to indicate those that do not represent developments in Minnesota during the last 20 years.

   .... Introduction of an income tax
   .... Great increase in the tourist industry
   .... Vigorous growth of consumer cooperatives
   .... Introduction of sales taxes
   .... Increased productivity in art and writing
   .... Marked increase in jobs placed under state civil service

In the following items place in the blank at the left the letter identifying the appropriate source of information or help that you would seek in each of the situations described.

[1] Eckert and Pace, *op. cit.*

146

.... To protest that your property has been overassessed
.... To protest against the licensing of a liquor store in your neighborhood
.... To obtain help in getting satisfaction from a company from which you ordered a cord of wood (128 cubic feet) but received only 90 cubic feet
.... To report that young couples were "necking" late at night in the park across the street from your house
.... To help you collect money for damages ($50) that some one has done to your car when neither party has insurance to cover the accident

A. City Engineer
B. Board of Park Commissioners
C. Board of Public Welfare
D. Police Department
E. City Attorney
F. Bureau of Licenses, Weights, and Measures
G. Board of Estimate and Taxation

From the standpoint of reliability, or consistency of measurement, these tests were quite satisfactory for the purposes for which they had been constructed. The fall reliability coefficients were .92 (Form A) and .91 (Form B), based on two hundred representative General College freshmen; for the spring retesting the coefficients were .93 (Form A) and .91 (Form B). Fall and spring results for the same students correlated to the extent of .75. Real differences in students' ranking at the beginning and the end of the year were, of course, to be expected because of variations in the character of their intervening school experiences. Covariance analyses revealed no significant difference due to the particular form of the test used, so that this factor could be disregarded in analyzing the achievement of various groups of students.

The pretest scores made by two groups of freshmen in 1939–40 — those who were enrolled in the socio-civic core courses in 1939–40 and those who were not — were very similar, as Figure 21 shows. In other words, these courses were not elected predominantly by students with superior backgrounds in the field or, on the other hand, by those who seemingly had the greatest

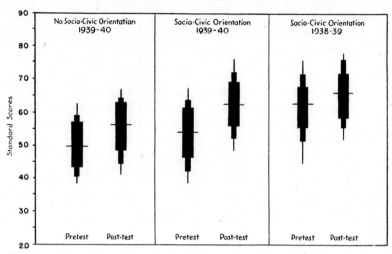

Figure 21. Scores of students who had taken socio-civic orientation courses and those who had not on the Socio-Civic Affairs Test. (See Figures 8 and 14 for explanation.)

need for this instruction because of gaps or inadequacies in their earlier training. This impressive lack of difference between the two groups poses an important question for general education: What types of students should be encouraged to take these basic orientation courses?

Men students showed a rather decisive superiority over women in their comprehension of and insight into the kinds of problems stated in this test. Since this same trend has appeared in numerous other studies, it suggests that in elementary and secondary school, as well as in out-of-school situations, boys are stimulated more effectively than girls to become interested in contemporary issues and problems. The present study reveals a difference so marked that in his knowledge of this particular area the typical General College man surpasses more than three fourths of all the women tested.

Figure 21 also indicates that most students made significant gains during this one year. How much young people in a different college environment, or out of school entirely, would gain on the same tests in a one-year period is of course unknown. Freshmen who did not take either of the core courses offered in the socio-civic area — Contemporary Society or Current History — approximated by the end of the year the precollege competency of liberal arts freshmen; apparently, then, the whole General College program contributed to these goals. The specific factors or experiences that helped to account for this marked gain ought to be identified and carefully studied, for if we can find out how to raise the level of understanding of the less promising students to that of the more able students, we shall have made a highly significant educational discovery.

Students who had taken courses in Current History or Contemporary Society made the largest gains on the test, surpassing by the end of the year the pretest performance of approximately 80 per cent of the entering freshmen. These gains were further explored through covariance analyses, which made it possible to adjust the final scores for differences in initial standing. These adjustments were made on the basis of pretest scores on the Socio-Civic Affairs Test and high school percentile ranks. The resulting F-ratios indicated that students in the socio-civic orientation courses had gained decisively more than those not enrolled. The data also revealed that the two core courses, Current History and Contemporary Society, contributed about equally to this particular type of outcome.

Other covariance analyses helped to answer the question of whether men or women students gained more in socio-civic understanding during one year of study. Although the men's scores decisively surpassed those of the women on both the pretests and the post-tests, the extent of gain made by the two sexes could not be differentiated. It would therefore seem that men and women profited almost equally, with respect to these particular outcomes, from the courses they had taken in the General College.

Similarly, since there was little difference in the information and insight gained by freshmen and by sophomores, we may conclude that a year's residence at either level results in about the same increase in the understanding of socio-civic problems. Social science courses taken by sophomores apparently continue and extend the same types of growth as are fostered by the two socio-civic orientation courses, which tend to be elected primarily by entering students.

The Wesley College Test of Social Terms, which probes students' understanding of common social and economic concepts, was also used in the present appraisal. Since this particular test was included each year in the General College entrance testing program, repetition of it two years later permitted a study of the gains students had made during this period. The typical sophomore student now achieved a score that placed him at the eightieth percentile of the entering freshman distribution. This gain was much too marked to be attributed solely to the students' previous acquaintance with the examination. Unfortunately, since pre- and post-test results were not available for other junior college populations, it could not be determined whether the General College gains were greater or smaller than those made by students elsewhere.

The contribution made by the core courses in this area to the students' understanding of social terms was then studied by covariance analyses. Final scores on the Wesley test were adjusted for initial differences in scores on the same test and on the Socio-Civic Affairs Test. When such corrections were made for differences in socio-civic background, young people in the orientation courses were discovered to have gained significantly more than other students. Again it appeared that the General College program had fulfilled in considerable degree the goals set for it.

The Cooperative Contemporary Affairs Test was the third examination used in this series. Since the nature of the test necessitates new editions each calendar year, it was impossible to administer the same test more than once. The results, however, revealed some exceedingly interesting facts about the emphasis placed on contemporary affairs in the General College program.

A comparison of the knowledge of current affairs possessed by General College sophomores and sophomores in colleges throughout the country is given in Figure 22. Despite the wide differences in general academic aptitude suggested by the fact that the typical General College student ranked at the twenty-second percentile of liberal arts college students and at the

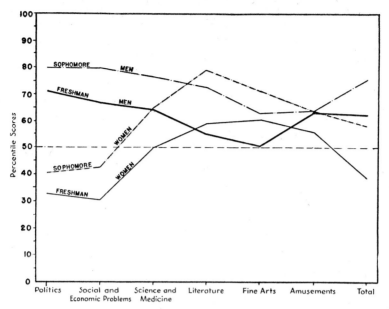

Figure 22. Scores of General College students on the Cooperative Contemporary Affairs Test. The percentile scores are based on national norms for college sophomores. Vertical distances are not comparable because a percentile rather than a sigma scale was used.

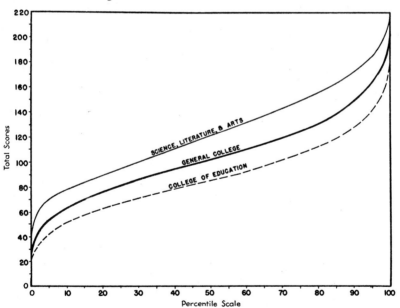

Figure 23. Scores of General College sophomores and other sophomore groups on the Cooperative Contemporary Affairs Test.

thirty-fifth percentile of junior college students on the American Council Psychological Examination, General College young people did more than simply hold their own on this test. General College sophomore men were superior to typical sophomores elsewhere on all six sections of the examination, and General College women on all but the political and economic sections. Though higher scores on this test may conceivably have indicated merely a better "headline" acquaintance with current happenings, at the very least General College students demonstrated a superior sensitivity to issues and personalities in the news, which was a basic aim of their instructors.

General College sophomores also showed up well when they were compared with sophomores in the other divisions of the University of Minnesota (Figure 23). Thus, as a group, they quite definitely outranked students in the College of Education's four-year curriculum, despite the superiority of the Education students with respect to high school rank and measured college aptitude. More striking is the comparison of the achievement of students in the General College and the College of Science, Literature, and the Arts on this test, also shown in Figure 23. The typical General College sophomore, whose high school percentile rank was only 31, as compared with a percentile rank of 93 for the average arts college sophomore, actually achieved a percentile score of 30 in the arts college sophomore distribution for this test. In other words, despite the fact that there was a difference of 62 percentile points on the general aptitude test, there was a difference of only 19 percentile points on the contemporary affairs test. The strong emphasis that the General College has placed on acquaintance with contemporary affairs thus produced a quality of performance far above what might have been predicted from general aptitude test results.

More exact comparisons between General College students and those enrolled in the College of Education and the College of Science, Literature, and the Arts were made by covariance techniques, which permitted adjustment of final scores for the wide initial differences between these groups in high school rank and scores on the American Council Psychological Examination.

This resulted in highly significant differences (F-ratios well beyond the 1 per cent level) for three of the four analyses made, with the results decisively favoring General College men and women over men and women enrolled in the College of Education, and General College women over the women enrolled in the College of Science, Literature, and the Arts. The difference was not significant for the men alone, though for the two sexes combined General College students made greater gains than arts college students did. These evidences clearly indicate that more deliberate and successful attention had been paid to this objective in the General College than in these other divisions.

On certain sections of this test, such as that on literature, General College students who had taken the socio-civic orientation courses could not be differentiated in their performance from other General College students, a fact that lends additional significance to the higher scores they made on sections directly related to these socio-civic courses (see Figure 24). Students

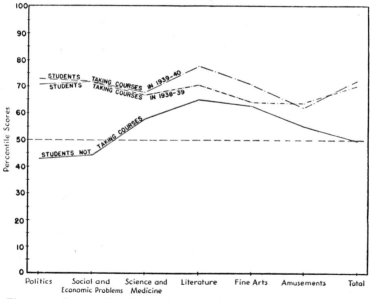

Figure 24. Scores of students who had taken the socio-civic orientation courses and those who had not on the Cooperative Contemporary Affairs Test. (See Figure 22 for explanation.)

who took Current History gained much more on the section on political events than did those who took the broader, more general course in Contemporary Society. This difference was not surprising in view of the fact that *Time* serves as the text for the Current History course. Students in these socio-civic orientation groups were distinctly superior to the typical General College students in their comprehension of social and economic problems.

In summary, therefore, results from these tests of basic facts and generalizations showed that tangible values accrued from membership in the General College. Students enrolled in this general education program showed substantial progress in their understanding of social trends and problems, and those who took courses specifically designed to contribute to these types of growth made the greatest gains.

CHANGES IN ATTITUDES TOWARD SOCIAL PROBLEMS

Another deep-seated concern of general education is the point of view that young people adopt toward social issues. Do they tend to become more genuinely liberal during the years they spend in college? Do the opinions they express give promise that they will act in a socially enlightened way when important choices present themselves?

The Pace Situations Test, designed to assess attitudes toward political, social, and economic problems,[2] was one of the measures used to identify these more elusive but highly critical outcomes. The Pace test was given to all entering freshmen in the fall of 1939 and to the same group the following spring.

According to results obtained from this test, a year's residence in the General College effected no essential modification of social and economic views, as may be seen in Figure 25. The very slight shift in the liberal direction suggested by this graph was not statistically significant. It would appear that social attitudes are so deeply implanted by the time young people come to college that instruction has little measurable effect.

[2] C. Robert Pace, "A Situations Test to Measure Social-Political-Economic Attitudes," *Journal of Social Psychology*, 11:369–81.

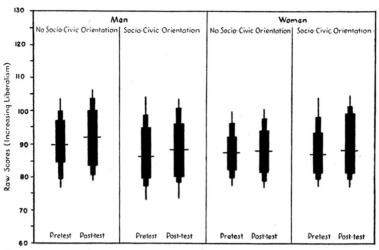

Figure 25. Scores of men and women who had taken the socio-civic orientation courses and those who had not on the Pace Situations Test. (See Figure 8 for explanation.)

Special studies made of the attitudes expressed by young people who took or did not take the socio-civic orientation courses revealed this fact even more vividly. Using covariance techniques to adjust for differences in initial scores on this test and on the Socio-Civic Affairs Test, to which attitudes might logically seem related, no differences were discovered at the end of the year between instructed and uninstructed students. In other words, membership in the socio-civic courses did not seem to modify or change students' points of view toward important contemporary problems.

Exactly the same lack of change was discovered for the Economic Conservatism section of the Minnesota Personality Scale. A firm adherence to the status quo was a social attitude as characteristic of students who had taken basic courses in the socio-civic area as it was of those who had had no special instruction, a fact revealed by the other covariance analyses. It is possible, of course, that these attitudes now rested on a more rational basis; the present data simply indicate that instruction in the socio-civic area did not noticeably modify either the points of view or the action tendencies of students toward specific social problems. Certainly on the basis of such evidence no one could fairly accuse the General College program either of turning students into radicals or of indoctrinating them in any particular social ideology.

On the Economic Conservatism section of the Minnesota Personality Scale it was possible to compare the attitudes expressed by General College students with those held by College of Education students who had also taken the test after two years of college study. Final scores were adjusted for initial differences in high school rank and general aptitude test scores, since precollege results were not available for this inventory. Even when such corrections were made, the two groups reached the end of the sophomore year with surprisingly similar attitudes. In other words, General College young people gave neither more nor less promise of enlightened social action than did other students. Granted that these particular tests are fallible indicators of changes in attitude, the results still represent a challenge to educators to discover how the schools may develop the "broader perspective on social problems" and "the deepened social consciousness" so often mentioned in statements of educational objectives.

PARTICIPATION IN SOCIO-CIVIC ACTIVITIES

Do young people who study social problems, who learn a great deal about their own communities, actually emerge from such courses with more serious reading interests, more educated tastes in radio programs, greater interest and participation in campus and community affairs? Unless they do, the chances of extending and applying the understandings developed in college courses to out-of-school situations would seem to be rather slim. Studies were therefore made, using analysis of variance and chi-square techniques, to determine the patterns of recreational interest and participation of, first, the total group of students and, second, students who took the core courses in the socio-civic area and those who did not.

In the General College freshman group as a whole, students at the end of the year showed tastes and participation patterns quite similar to those exhibited at their entrance to college. They now engaged a little more in general conversation and discussion, but the quality of their reading, radio listening, or socio-civic participation had apparently not improved.

More impressive evidence that the program exerted little influence on students' participation in activities was discovered when those who took work in this area were compared with those who did not. The former group, for example, attended student forums, university convocations, and campus conferences on social problems no more frequently than other students, nor did they belong to more campus organizations or listen to serious radio programs or read different magazines than young people not enrolled in these courses. The very occasional differences that did appear favored only one of the core courses, Current History, indicating that the students who took that course were somewhat more interested than the others in the university newsreel theater, news magazines, and news commentators.

We need to bear in mind, of course, that the effects of such instruction may not be perceived for a considerable time. A person who studies art may begin to paint pictures immediately, but a student who has taken courses in economics, sociology, or political science cannot immediately start to pay taxes, canvass for political candidates, or coach plays in the neighborhood community house. However, it might have been expected that the impact of the General College socio-civic courses would have been perceptible in the areas of reading, radio listening, and campus activities.

Finally, the civic activities and interests of former General College students were investigated. Despite the fact that many of these young people had received the Associate of Arts degree, once they had left college their activities could in no way be distinguished from those of students who had dropped out before graduation. Likewise, these former students exhibited patterns of responses almost identical with those of students still attending the General College. The only significant exception was that young people who had been out of school for some years reported more radio listening and more leisure-time reading than present students did. The passage of years had apparently not given them a more mature social philosophy or led them to identify themselves more actively with civic affairs in the community. Again this may not be due entirely to disinterest in these affairs, but to the fact that all their energies, during the first years out of college, were absorbed in career and family.

The socio-civic activities of these former General College students, especially those who had received the Associate in Arts degree, were then critically compared with those reported by young adults who had withdrawn from other colleges of the university after a comparable period of residence and who had been out of school the same length of time. Again, amazingly similar interests and activities were revealed — to suggest once more the small influence of any school environment on out-of-school activities. On more than a hundred identical items the few differences that emerged pointed to slightly greater interest and slightly more participation on the part of students from other colleges. Among both groups interests were directed rather toward large national issues than toward specific local problems, and participation was chiefly limited to quite routine activities. For example, less than a fifth of these former students had signed petitions to government officials or campaigned for election candidates; fewer than a tenth had written letters to government officials, attended meetings of political clubs or of law-making bodies, tried to influence the passage of a law, or attended community forums. Only one young adult in forty had ever served on a committee dealing with civic problems. Lacking comparable figures for adults in general, or for college populations outside Minnesota, it is difficult to interpret these figures. Certainly the amount of participation seems disappointing in view of the long years of schooling these young people had. The majority of college-trained adults, in common with many other people, are apparently quite willing to let someone else take care of the social order, as long as their own security is not affected. Though another world war has shaken this complacent attitude, it remains for the schools to find as strong a motivation for peacetime tasks.

SOCIO-CIVIC COMPETENCE

The value of General College courses in helping a young person to understand the meaning of social, political, and economic problems was quite emphatically acknowledged by two former students in every three—many more than the group who endorsed statements concerning the value of General College courses in the solution of personal, home and family, and vocational problems. This is undoubtedly due in some measure to the fact that more students elect courses in the social studies than in any other field. Among the specific courses that seemed to assist most in clarifying social concepts were Current History, mentioned by one student in four, and Formation of Public Opinion, Social Trends and Problems, and Our Economic Life, each mentioned by approximately one in every six.[3] Several comments will illustrate how these courses contributed to socio-civic orientation:

"Social Trends and Problems gave me a wider view of social problems and how we are directly or indirectly responsible for social maladjustment."

"Formation of Public Opinion brought me to realize the dangers of propaganda. Economic Life has also helped in various cases."

"Formation of Public Opinion and Current Affairs made me a faithful reader of *Time*. After reading this magazine through each week, a fellow knows pretty well what is going on in this world."

"Social Problems and Economics, because they deal with and give a background on such matters, making them easier to understand when we find them in books, outside, and in newspapers."

"Current Affairs helped me to weigh news reports and to look into their background. All courses in the history and government group have proved to be valuable because of their contemporary views and considerations."

SUMMARY

Although the picture of the interests, understandings, and activities of General College young people in socio-civic affairs is disheartening in some respects, it is distinctly encouraging in others. Evidently a college that offers courses in contemporary

[3] The course Contemporary Society, being a recent addition to the program, had not been taken by these former students.

problems can definitely assist students in attaining clearer social concepts, in reaching a better understanding of political and economic issues, and in becoming more intimately acquainted with contemporary happenings. This emphasis on current affairs may so pervade the entire program that these goals are implemented through many courses.

Yet a superior grasp of these problems apparently does not bring about more enlightened attitudes, as social attitudes are at present measured. All the experiences provided by the college have apparently not effected a genuine reorientation of the group to pressing social and political issues, although many students were unquestionably stimulated by these courses. Likewise, actual participation, at least within the time period included in the present study, does not seem to be significantly influenced by residence in the college, nor is it apparently affected by special study in the socio-civic area. Although such courses certainly should not be expected to build all the traits of citizenship desired by any college, there is cause for concern when students who have been especially sensitized to the opportunities for activity in campus and community affairs show almost the same lack of participation as those who have not had specific instruction.

Finally, perhaps the most fundamentally disquieting revelation is the fact that it is impossible to distinguish, on the basis of their out-of-school problems, their social attitudes, or their socio-civic activities, between students who have dropped out of a traditional program of education and those who have completed the two-year general education program. Although few conclusions can be drawn without more information concerning the goals that motivate the selection of one activity rather than another and concerning the values derived from such experiences, the present findings suggest that there exist certain dynamics of action not yet touched by even a highly progressive educational program.

CHAPTER 11

Students' Attitudes toward the General College Program

Any experimental college must continually check the effectiveness of its own program by finding out what students and former students consider to be its present strengths and weaknesses. This does not imply that young people's opinions should be used as a sole, or even a primary, basis for judging the success of the college. The popularity of a curriculum is no convincing indication that it is building satisfactory educational outcomes. Experiences that have important implications for students' future living may conceivably be those to which they attach little immediate worth. It is reasonable to suppose, however, that young people will gain far more from experiences that appear to them to be meaningful and valuable in the immediate present than from those that hold only a promise of remote and somewhat intangible returns. The ultimate test of the success of a college program admittedly and rightly lies in actual changes in the thinking and behavior of youth; therefore studies of students' attitudes are of value chiefly as they reveal the extent to which young people are now actively appraising these experiences and thereby becoming more keenly aware of the contributions made by the college to their own growth and development.

In this reported appraisal it seemed highly important to find out how young people who sat in General College classes, those who became intimately acquainted with faculty members and administrative officers, those who were known as "the General College students" by other students on the campus, judged the worth of their training. Their opinions about specific college services and about the program as a whole were therefore explored in a variety of ways. More than 1500 students and former students expressed the opinions that are summarized in this chapter.

After the four orientation courses had been offered for a single quarter, the first reactions of students to them were obtained through a check list, filled out anonymously and involving many specific comparisons between orientation and subject-matter courses. More than eight hundred replies were received and the various opinions and comments analyzed according to the particular combinations of courses elected by these students.

Furthermore, a cross section of opinions concerning the entire program was obtained through interviews with more than a hundred students in the spring of 1939. They were given an opportunity to discuss the program as freely as they wished and their answers gave important but exceedingly subtle evidences, revealed in the emotional toning of students' remarks and their readiness to open new topics for discussion — another distinct advantage of the interview approach. These discussions, conducted by the director of the appraisal studies and a graduate student in counseling and psychometrics, ranged in length from fifteen minutes to an hour and a half, depending on the interviewee's willingness to talk and his ability to supply pertinent information. The average conference lasted about half an hour. Further interviews were held with General College students in October and November 1939, when a hundred representative freshmen stated the reasons why they had elected the courses in which they were then enrolled and their present attitudes toward those courses. Some months later thirty students, chosen because of the outstanding superiority of their fall-quarter work, were interviewed to obtain their appraisal of the General College program.

Also in the spring of that year the Committee on Educational Research canvassed opinions of the 1938 Minnesota high school graduates who had entered Minnesota colleges concerning the values of their first year of college work, using a carefully formulated eight-page questionnaire for this purpose.[1] Fewer

[1] G. Lester Anderson, "The Reactions of College Freshmen to Their First Year of College Experience," in *Studies in Higher Education*, Biennial Report of the University Committee on Educational Research, 1938–40, pp. 41–51.

General College freshmen responded (207 students) than had been expected, though the percentage of response was as good as that for other colleges. Those who did reply seemed thoroughly characteristic of the total General College group in ability and achievement. Extensive duplication in the items of the interview and the questionnaire, even though they had been selected independently, permitted many checks on the consistency of General College students' opinions.

Many students who filled out this freshman questionnaire reappraised their college experiences a year later by means of a similar, though shortened, questionnaire. Only 90 General College sophomores replied, since half of the original group had already left the university. Nevertheless the ideas expressed by these sophomores agreed closely with other evidences of student opinion.

The General College Student Council made a final and more inclusive survey in the spring of 1940. Several months earlier the students had been invited by the director of curriculum revision to assist in identifying the strengths and weaknesses of present General College courses and to offer suggestions for the further development of the curriculum. In consequence, council officers worked closely with the faculty and with the evaluator in framing a four-page questionnaire, phrasing and rephrasing each item in an effort to invite reasoned and thoroughly honest reactions. Of the 635 students originally selected for this particular survey, more than 75 per cent responded, or more than half of all students enrolled in the General College during the spring quarter of 1940.

ATTITUDES TOWARD GENERAL COLLEGE COURSES

Since General College courses differ impressively from those given in typical high schools or colleges, what the students consider to be the tangible benefits or liabilities of this new curriculum constitutes highly significant information. Broad questions concerning the interest and the value of General College courses were often followed by such specific inquiries as "In which course did you have the best lectures?" "In which course was there the best general morale or interest on the part of the students?" or "In which course did you work the hardest?" The replies indicated that almost no student felt any hesitancy in sharing his convictions, however iconoclastic they might be. This in itself would seem to indicate a wholesome, experimental attitude toward the program.

TABLE 7. THE TEN HIGHEST RANKING GENERAL COLLEGE COURSES ON THE BASIS OF ESTIMATED VALUE AND INTEREST *

Value			Interest		
Course	N	Rank	Course	N	Rank
Human Biology	184	1	Human Biology	186	1
Business Mathematics ...	72	2	Physical Science	102	2
Practical Applications of Psychology	203	3	Radio Workshop	49	3
Radio Workshop	49	4	Practical Applications of Psychology	207	4
Physical Science	100	5	Business Mathematics ...	74	5
Selecting and Maintaining a Home	57	6	Art Today	89	6
Speech Laboratory	98	7	International Relations ..	112	7
Clothing Selection	68	8.5	Clothing Selection	65	8
Conversation Laboratory	32	8.5	Film and Drama	61	9
Functions and Problems of Government	89	10	Social Trends and Problems	119	10

* From the Student Council questionnaire. N represents the number of students enrolled in the course during the year who answered this particular question (495 students returned the questionnaire). The figures were used in adjusting student ratings of course popularity for differences in the actual enrollments in these courses.

A general picture of these opinions is shown in Table 7. The courses that impressed students as having the greatest positive strength were Human Biology, Practical Applications of Psychology, Speech, Physical Science, and Business Mathematics. None of the orientation courses ranked among the highest ten with respect to either interest or value. This was not surprising, since the orientation courses were comparatively new in the General College curriculum, as they are in the whole field of general education, and therefore might not have had sufficient time to establish themselves. There were nevertheless striking variations in the popularity of these orientation courses. Current

History, for example, lagged only slightly behind the courses in government in estimated interest and value; Home Life Orientation, on the other hand, was quite consistently near the bottom of all lists. Perhaps this difference is due in part to the fact that Current History deviated much less impressively than Home Life Orientation from the kinds of courses to which students had become accustomed in high school. Whatever factors account for the ratings, it seems important to recognize such a difference in attitude. Ratings derived from the interview studies and the Committee on Educational Research survey of freshman adjustment resulted in a ranking of courses almost identical to that given in Table 7.

Explanations given by students for their ratings suggest certain bases on which the courses were evaluated. Illustrative of the comments students frequently expressed concerning courses they judged to be of distinct value are the following:

"I like the subject-matter organization, detail, and the fact that this course has somewhat technical materials."

"Has more immediate and practical applications than other courses; problems of health are important to everyone."

"More direct benefit because of practical content — good for everyday living as well as vocational preparation."

"Only class conducted in businesslike manner; teacher tried to get materials across in S.L.A. fashion."

"Helped to build up straighter thinking habits in my other courses; I find myself constantly applying there what I've learned in Psychology."

"One course I really got something from; got more real knowledge than from any course I took. Conduct was excellent in that course."

For those courses that were looked upon with little favor, criticisms centered around a lack of challenge in the subject matter. Students again and again implied by their comments that the materials were perhaps too obvious to require college study.

"Lack of difficulty — would like a stiffer course and one that does not overlap so much with what I already know. And I have very different opinions on certain issues from those presented in class."

"I doubt whether there is any content — could be mimeographed in a few pages."

"All obvious — wouldn't have to go to class. This isn't economics but keeping of bees, cows. Boring."

"Not much to be got out of it; knew much of materials presented in class before I took the course."

In the Student Council study more specific criticisms and suggestions were obtained by asking questions concerning the suitability of the content, the instructor's presentation, the amount of outside work demanded, and the types of examinations employed to measure achievement. Each student criticized only one designated course, the name of the course being written on his individual questionnaire. Although only a small group of students — an average of fourteen — so appraised each course, their comments concerning the character of instruction offered surprisingly close confirmation of the ratings of courses given by much larger groups of students. Courses that were well liked were commended for their clear organization, interesting content, and the challenge they provided to further study. Courses held in lowest repute were most often scored for the elementary nature of the material, the evident overlapping with other courses, and the poor discipline in the classroom.

Another way of checking on students' opinions of the present curriculum was to discover what alterations they might have made in their program of study if they could have re-registered for courses. In three of the interview and questionnaire studies the students listed courses that they would have omitted and courses they now wished that they had included in their General College program. After each nomination or rejection of a course they indicated the reasons that supposedly motivated their decision.

The data from this study agreed thoroughly with other findings concerning the popularity of General College courses. Courses with which students were apparently most dissatisfied were General Arts Orientation,[2] Home Life Orientation, and Survey of Recreational Activities, each mentioned by about a

[2] This was a new course, taught for the first time during the year in which this appraisal study was completed. It should not be confused with Art Today, which ranked among the more popular courses.

fifth of the students enrolled in them. About one student in six also expressed discontent with the courses in Individual Orientation; United States in World Civilization; Renting, Buying, and Building a Home; and Social Relations of Physical Science. Illustrative of the comments made by students in singling out these courses are the following statements:

"I am not learning a thing. It is by far too general and haphazard."

"The lectures are usually dull and uninteresting, when they could be presented in an intensely interesting manner."

"I have had the same principles of history twice before."

"Not interesting; poor material. We are supposed to be college students, not high school youngsters."

"The . . . course is practically worthless in that it informs in a minor degree exactly the same things I get out of other classes. Furthermore, it may have intentions to orient an individual, but it has fallen short. Is given in a slipshod manner, including many unnecessary details that as a whole are worthless and impossible to judge an examination on."

"The lectures were crowded with uninteresting and unnecessary dates and figures."

"Anyone knows what is taught here, and there are continual repetitions."

"Silly course. It's a natural adjustment and no schooling on the subject will change anything in this line."

The courses that young people wished they had taken were the same courses, by and large, that students who had taken them valued highly. Human Biology headed the list, specified by 10 per cent of those not enrolled in the course; Practical Applications of Psychology was a close second; Speech Laboratory and Writing Laboratory were also mentioned by more than one student in every twelve as being definitely desirable. The total number of students who specified courses they would like to have included was significantly smaller than the number who expressed dissatisfaction with one or more of their present courses. The reasons given by students who would have liked work in a particular field agree closely with opinions expressed by young people actually enrolled in such courses.

"Because everyone that takes it enjoys it."

"Very practical and factual."

"Speech is fundamental in any walk of life. A person is easily judged by his English, socially and at work."

"Gives one a knowledge of things that would be helpful in teaching and speaking."

"Speech Laboratory would help me break down some of my inferiority complex."

"I believe it would be beneficial to me in the kind of work I want to get into."

"I believe these are practical courses and offer something in the way of an essential contribution to further academic work."

ATTITUDES TOWARD TEACHING MATERIALS, PROCEDURES, AND DEGREE REQUIREMENTS

Whenever inclusive survey courses are offered, the problem of duplication with previous educational experiences tends to become acute. This is especially true when a curriculum is organized on two different bases — that of functional-need courses, which command facts and principles in subject-matter fields so as to clarify the basic problems of immediate and personal living, and that of survey courses, which attempt to provide a general view of major subject-matter fields. Such groups of courses must inevitably overlap. Particularly in the functional-need group the nature of the topics discussed must also result in much repetition of materials encountered out of school through such sources as the press, the radio, and motion pictures. The more realistically these courses seek to prepare young people for their out-of-school responsibilities, the more serious must this problem of articulation with other experiences become. All duplication is certainly not undesirable, its value depending on whether sheer repetition is involved or whether the experiences serve to extend and enrich meanings already comprehended. Intelligent reinforcement can only come, however, as an instructor is aware of the understandings and attitudes that his students bring with them or that they are simultaneously acquiring in other courses or extracurricular experiences.

Little duplication was specifically noted by General College students between their present courses and those taken in high school, despite the repeatedly expressed opinions that they knew in advance much of the material presented in some courses.

Among the various General College courses, overlapping was indicated most frequently between Individual Orientation and Practical Applications of Psychology, between Individual Orientation and Human Development, between Home Life Orientation and Human Development, and between Contemporary Society and Social Trends and Problems. Such duplication apparently lowered the interest and value of such courses, for students who took any of these pairs rated both of them less favorably than students who took either course alone. As many of the previous comments show, sheer repetition of materials was the most serious single charge leveled against General College offerings. Although this duplication was mentioned frequently, it may be questioned whether or not this is as serious a defect as the opposite condition found in so many colleges — the general lack of integration among subject-matter courses.

The amount of time General College students reported that they spent in study would seem to indicate that they were not overburdened with their academic work. A great many students remarked, both in the interviews and in free comments on questionnaires, that the absence of day-by-day requirements in most courses had led them to work less systematically than in high school, a feeling that students in other colleges would probably share. They admitted that their studying was largely concentrated around midquarters, finals, and deadline dates for book reports or term papers. In consequence most of them could not estimate the amount of time spent each week in studying or reading outside the classroom. But again and again these young people observed that most of the courses did not demand sustained work and that a raising of scholastic standards would both motivate General College students and increase the college's prestige in the eyes of other university students.

The fragmentary and often unsatisfactory reading materials available for general education courses have presented to faculty members a serious instructional problem. The most appropriate reading is often found in current periodicals, and two or three library copies of each can hardly serve the two or three hundred students enrolled in certain courses. But when General College students were questioned concerning such problems, only an occasional individual mentioned a dearth of appropriate materials, a fact that suggests rather casual use of library resources. Again this finding is certainly not typical of the General College alone, for in every school there must exist a startling disparity between what instructors assign and what students actually do.

Since transfer to other colleges or graduation from the General College depends primarily upon fulfilling comprehensive-examination requirements, students' opinions of these tests were

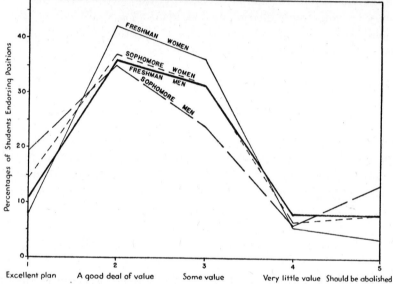

Figure 26. General College students' evaluation of the comprehensive-examination requirement for graduation.

also canvassed. Reactions of nearly five hundred General College students revealed considerable unanimity of opinion; men and women and freshmen and sophomores viewed this requirement as moderately desirable, as may be seen in Figure 26. Marked enthusiasm was lacking, and so also was any crystallized antagonism. The few students who strongly objected to comprehensive examinations favored using as criteria either course marks or shorter and more frequent tests. While no objective data are available to check the hypothesis, discussions with students during this two-year period suggested a trend toward more whole-hearted acceptance of comprehensive examinations. Clarification of these requirements, the planning of study programs on a yearly instead of a quarterly basis, and the preparation of a student handbook explaining the nature of the tests undoubtedly helped to account for this change.

ATTITUDES TOWARD COUNSELING AND ADVISORY SERVICES

The heart of any general education plan must lie in an effective counseling service. Certain basic objectives of general education, such as that of understanding one's personal needs and characteristics, probably depend for their realization less upon courses of any sort than upon sympathetic yet thoroughly objective and realistic personnel services. The individual student — his activities, problems, and needs — must be the unifying center of any meaningful program of general education.

At the General College two types of counseling are offered. The whole faculty assists in the making of study programs, each staff member advising from thirty to sixty students about their selection of courses and their preparation for the comprehensive examinations. A central counseling staff coordinates these faculty efforts and also furnishes considerable assistance to students on registration problems. Its major concern, however, is to help students to analyze and solve their broader educational, personal, and vocational problems. Though the teaching staff and administrators also deal with many matters of adjustment and social relationships, the student is ordinarily referred to the counseling office for more thorough advisement.

Among the first problems investigated in connection with General College counseling were the extent and character of the aid that faculty members gave the students. Questions were included in the interviews or inventories to find out how often each student had seen a faculty adviser, on what kinds of problems, and with how much satisfaction. The median number of conferences these students reported that they had had with faculty advisers during one year was 3.5 each. It is interesting to note that only 10 per cent said that they had had fewer than two conferences a year with their faculty adviser, whereas a third of the others reported at least four conferences, or more than one a quarter. This does not include the number of conferences these same students may have had with members of the central counseling service, a point to be discussed later.

This amount of attention from faculty advisers was well beyond that reported by students in any other college of the university. For example, four times as many General College as arts college students reported conferences held during the year at their advisers' request, and more than twice as many General College as arts college students reported such conferences held at their own request. The difference in the amount of faculty attention received by General College students and those enrolled in smaller liberal arts colleges throughout the state was not as striking, yet General College young people still showed a definite advantage on this point.

More than 75 per cent of the General College students believed that faculty members, through these conferences, had helped them *very much* or *much;* less than 5 per cent indicated *hardly any* or *none* as a fair characterization of how much these services had meant to them personally. The help of parents, brothers, sisters, or friends on such problems was much less frequently recognized. Although General College students felt that Freshman Week activities had been of some real value, they ranked these activities well below faculty assistance in the contribution made to their orientation and adjustment in college.

From the survey of freshman adjustment carried out by the Committee on Educational Research it was found that the problems General College students discussed with faculty members centered chiefly around personal strengths and weaknesses as these affect vocational choice, the quality of their college work, the kind and number of courses needed for certain occupations, and the specific courses necessary to meet transfer requirements.[3] The topic which students showed the greatest eagerness to dis-

[3] In another volume of this series (Williams, *These We Teach*) the counseling problems presented by General College students are discussed in considerable detail.

cuss and which, these replies indicated, was not so frequently considered by the advisers was "What's the matter with me in general?" Other items that showed some still unsatisfied interest were how to get over being shy, how to meet and become friends with students of the opposite sex, and how to get invited to join a club or fraternity.

As might be expected from the preceding figures on the greater frequency of conferences for General College than for arts college students, General College young people discussed many more problems with their advisers. When the specific topics were surveyed, the greatest differences occurred on items concerning factors in vocational choice and concerning the educational training appropriate for a chosen career. There was much less distinction between these two groups in their reported discussions of such topics as study habits, membership in a club or fraternity, misunderstandings with instructors, or living conditions. Because General College students had had many more opportunities to discuss their academic and personal problems, far fewer students in this group checked topics that they wanted to discuss with faculty members but had not done so. It was interesting to note that the topics that arts college students had most desired to discuss with someone actually involved the same vocational problems that had claimed first attention in General College students' conferences.

More than nine out of every ten General College students said they had taken tests before or during their registration period, and two thirds of all those tested said that they had received some interpretation of the results. With only a few exceptions these students felt that suitable implications had been drawn with respect to their own educational and vocational plans. In this respect they again differed significantly from the arts college students, almost half of whom had received no test interpretations. About 20 per cent of the General College young people stated that someone on the college staff had told them that they should make an outstanding or better than average scholastic record; double that number (40 per cent) had been warned that they might have difficulty in making a satisfactory scholastic record in college. These percentages were, as one might expect, almost exactly reversed for the arts college students.

There was one other notable difference between the General College and arts college groups in this area of faculty counseling, and that concerned the attention that classroom instructors had given to students' interests, vocational choices, or avocational activities. General College students endorsed to a significantly greater extent than arts college students each of the five statements that reflected genuine concern on the part of the faculty for such problems. On certain items three times as many General College as arts college students checked the statement, impressive evidence of the personnel point of view that pervades the classrooms as well as the counseling offices of the General College.

Almost two fifths of the five hundred students included in the General College Student Council's survey reported that they had made no use that year of the special counseling services. Inasmuch as the counseling staff has always held the point of view that use of these advisory services should be on a voluntary basis, the significant fact undoubtedly is that three fifths of all General College students actually did use these resources. Those who had gone to the counseling service were deeply appreciative of the special help they had received. Of all students who had had any conferences with the members of the special counseling service, more than two thirds rated highly the value of the advice they had received, endorsing the top two positions on a five-point scale provided for this purpose. In addition to these very favorable general ratings, students also gave a great many vivid and impressive illustrations of the value of this special service in helping them to make appropriate vocational choices, to plan their further education, and to adjust themselves better to personal or family problems.

ATTITUDES TOWARD THE PROGRAM AS A WHOLE

Why students come to the General College and what they feel they are really deriving from their stay must be known to interpret correctly their evaluations of various aspects of the program. The extent to which young people feel that their general expectations have been realized must surely color all their more specific reactions.

The kinds of knowledge, understanding, and skill that young people had expected to gain from a first year in college and the kinds they thought they had actually received were canvassed through the Committee on Educational Research freshman questionnaire. The most insistent demands that General College young people made upon the college were for assistance in making wise occupational choices, in preparing for specific vocations, in training to think clearly about problems, in understanding their personal assets and liabilities, and in gaining greater facility in spoken and written expression. Yet it was on these particular points that the gaps appeared largest between what they wanted and what they thought college had given them, as may be seen in Table 8. General College students, in common with students in other divisions of the university, were apparently very eager to find out a great deal more than they now knew concerning their own patterns of abilities and interests and what implications lay in these patterns for vocational training and placement.[4]

When the responses given by those who had completed their freshman year in the College of Science, Literature, and the Arts were compared with these opinions expressed by General College freshmen, certain extremely interesting differences appeared, as a survey of Table 8 indicates. The liberal arts group showed on the whole a very similar patterning of interests, especially the same deep-seated concern for vocational readiness. On only three of the twenty items included in the original list were differences between the two groups significant at the 1 per cent level, in each case indicating a greater desire on the part of General College students for increased knowledge, skill, or understanding in a specified area.

In the belief that they had actually attained these desired goals, liberal arts freshmen lagged seriously behind General College freshmen. The most impressive differences, in every case favoring the General College group, occurred on the following items:

[4] Anderson, "Reactions of Minnesota College Freshmen," p. 47.

TABLE 8. COMPARISON OF 989 ARTS COLLEGE AND 207 GENERAL COLLEGE FRESHMEN WITH RESPECT TO DESIRED INCREASES IN KNOWLEDGE, UNDERSTANDING, AND SKILL, AND TO THE ACTUAL REALIZATION OF THESE DESIRES

Items*	Desired Increases			Actual Increases		
	Percentages		CR	Percentages		CR
	S.L.A.	G.C.		S.L.A.	G.C.	
To learn how to make a wise occupational choice	72	74	0.59	23	56	8.92
To learn how to prepare for the vocation of your choice	73	65	2.22	34	51	4.47
To learn about whole fields or areas of knowledge like science or the social studies	33	27	1.75	21	29	2.35
To learn how to think clearly, to meet a problem and follow it to a right conclusion	63	64	0.27	35	43	2.11
To learn how to choose leisure-time activities	29	31	0.57	19	32	3.71
To know and understand your own emotions and feelings	37	48	2.89	21	40	5.28
To know and understand the pressing social and economic problems of America	42	42	0.00	25	44	5.14
To know and understand world events, issues, and pressing problems	47	47	0.00	31	48	4.47
To understand why people act as they do	48	50	0.52	22	51	7.84
To know what your strengths, weaknesses, and limitations are	63	64	0.27	24	45	5.68
To know how new discoveries, inventions, etc., may affect us	21	30	2.65	11	26	4.55
To discover new interests	47	49	0.52	25	36	3.24
To know what is meant by the scientific point of view	22	29	2.06	22	33	3.14
To learn how to talk to others clearly and effectively	64	64	0.00	30	45	4.05
To learn how to be a more intelligent shopper	21	30	2.65	13	29	4.85
To learn how to enjoy the various arts	41	34	1.94	30	41	2.97

* Only those items that showed differences significant at the 5 per cent level in either column have been included in this table.

"To learn how to make a wise occupational choice," "To under-stand why people act as they do," "To know what your strengths, weaknesses, and limitations are," "To know and understand your own emotions and feelings," and "To know and understand the pressing social and economic problems of America." Whether General College freshmen actually increased their understand-ing of such problems to this extent or whether they had simply become more aware that these *were* important problems for

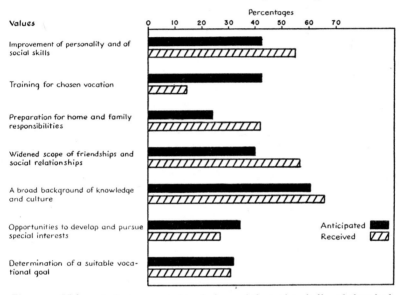

Figure 27. Values students expected to derive and those they believed they had actually derived from the General College program.

them, at least they completed the year far more convinced than were arts college students that the training they had received had been meaningful in terms of out-of-school needs and demands.

In the General College Student Council questionnaire an ef-fort was made to find out in what broad areas students had espe-cially desired help and to what extent residence in the General College had met these sensed needs. As is indicated in Figure 27, most students thought the greatest benefit they were obtain-ing from their college attendance was a broad background of knowledge and culture, although they also stressed the social advantages of an education. The most outstanding discrepancy between what students hoped for and what they thought they had actually obtained occurred on an item concerning job preparation; 43 per cent said they had wanted help on this problem, and only 15 per cent believed they had received it during their one or two years in the General College.[5] The general consistency in the direction of these results seems to be the most important finding, for it reveals the unsatisfied needs of many young people with respect to vocational preparation.

When students were given an opportunity to suggest desirable additions to the General College program, more than two thirds made no suggestions, indicating either that they were completely satisfied with the program as it was or that they had not considered possible alterations. Personal interviews with students supplied the principal reason for this attitude — the fact that many of them looked upon their General College experience as a rather transitory one.

Those who did suggest new offerings mentioned two general groups of courses. More than 60 per cent of the desired courses were academic offerings, such as courses in foreign languages, mathematics, and laboratory science that students felt might assist them later in other colleges of the university. On the other hand, students who hoped to get jobs immediately after leaving the General College were especially insistent that definite vocational training be provided, chiefly in accounting, typing, and salesmanship. Although most jobs may actually require only a short training period just preceding employment, the fact remains that a great many young people believe that the school ought to supply specific job preparation. Either such training ought to be given in the school or the understandings and attitudes of young people toward vocational problems ought to be

[5] These figures are considerably lower than those reported in Table 8, a difference due in part to differences in the context and directions of the two questionnaires. In the Committee on Educational Research questionnaire the students were requested to rate every item according to the amount of help they had received, whereas in the Student Council questionnaire they checked only those items that represented definite values accruing from General College residence. Since job preparation is not one of the primary objectives of the General College, many students omitted it in filling out the latter questionnaire.

so reoriented that they may see more clearly the contribution of a general education to the efficiency and enjoyment of their future careers.

After students have spent a year or two in the General College, what values do they attach to their experience? Do they leave the college with a conviction that they are well equipped for out-of-school tasks or with a feeling that the time has been largely wasted? Although some young people might not have pondered such questions, many possessed clearly defined and interesting convictions about the worth of this general education program.

One approach used in the interviews with students to obtain evidence on these points was to ask whether the student would recommend the General College to a younger brother or sister or a friend who had abilities and interests similar to his own. Despite the values attributed by many students to their General College experience, less than 10 per cent of the young people interviewed were ready to recommend the college without qualifications. Illustrative of the comments made by the most enthusiastic students are the following:

"Very much. A general education is the first thing a student should have, to learn to grow up before entering a professional school."

"Yes, I think it teaches things everyone needs to know."

"Yes, it initiates you gradually into a university form of curriculum and helps you to make a vocational choice. Gives you a lot of valuable information for general living."

About three students in every ten thought the program suitable for certain types of young people. Some of these students apparently had overlooked the directions that asked each one to assume that the young person had abilities and interests similar to his own. If they had done so their recommendations might not have been hedged with so many qualifications, the most frequent of which appear in the following comments:

"I would advise it definitely, except for extremely able people who should begin strenuous mental work immediately."

"It depends on his goal. If he hasn't got his feet on the ground

in high school, let him come here by all means. This is good for anyone. My only objection is the time element in transferring."

"For a person who is doubtful, this is the best place to come. If
he is definitely interested and has *abilities*, let him go to another unit
for appropriate training."

Immaturity, a poor quality of high school work, and a need
for gaining social poise and broadened experience (claimed most
often by graduates of small high schools) were other reasons
given for advising a young person to enter the General College
instead of one of the other divisions of the university.

For another two students in ten, the sex of the advisee would
determine whether or not he should enter the college. For girls
the General College program was deemed of considerable value;
for boys a more direct and specific vocational training was recommended.

"Not a boy. There is nothing in the General College you can get
a job with. I'd send a girl unless she was entering nursing or some
job like that."

"Sister, yes — for this program is good for any girl. A brother,
no — unless he were undecided or only had one or two years to go
to college."

A few students were too uncertain to venture any sort of
opinion on this question.

"I'm not certain, for it would depend on my brother's or sister's
interests and on whether the General College would contribute to
his or her vocational goal. If they hadn't decided, I'd probably say
yes."

"Uncertain — depends on the kind of person he is. If he were like
me, I'd possibly send him here."

The remaining students, constituting three out of every ten
of those interviewed, were against advising entrance to the General College. In a few cases this was because some other college
would be their first recommendation.

"Not unless he had to. S.L.A.[6] is a straight route. Transfer problems are the chief hindering factor, for how are General College
courses evaluated elsewhere?"

"No, I'd advise them to go to S.L.A. They would be too limited

[6] The College of Science, Literature, and the Arts.

here, gaining too much practical knowledge and not enough cultural knowledge."

Other students who withheld recommendations were more definitely unfavorable in their attitudes, as the following comments show:

"Not unless it was absolutely necessary. You can get same values from S.L.A. and at the same time get information that will result in monetary value sooner or later."

"No, mainly because other colleges do more good for you. No one does any work. They are always horsing around, and the morale of college is low. My friends don't know I'm in the General College. When they joke, I don't say anything, just sit back and laugh."

"It would be a waste of time. Even if they didn't know what they wanted, they should go to S.L.A., and they'd really get something."

"General College is a great place if one has money enough to throw a few years away."

Students were also asked whether they thought that they would be willing to reenter the college if they were again confronted with this decision. "If you had known as much at the time of registration as you do now concerning your present year's program (and had not been required to come to the General College) would you have entered voluntarily?" Replies to this question resulted in a more favorable evaluation of the General College experience. Possibly the college's lack of academic prestige loomed larger when students debated sending another member of their family than when they simply reconsidered their own entrance, since many had undoubtedly become convinced of their own scholastic handicaps.

About 15 per cent of the interviewed students showed a definite enthusiasm for the program, indicating by their comments that the college had so met their individual needs that they would without question have re-registered there if again confronted with this choice. Typical of this point of view are the following statements:

"I am glad I came here because I got more good out of this college than I would anywhere else. I needed general training. But I resented having to come here. Last year it was held up to me as a place where tramp athletes go."

"I would come here if I had to decide again. Not only do I like it much better, but I have received much more individual attention here."

"I've learned more practical things, more than I'd get in S.L.A. in ten years."

Another 30 per cent agreed that they would come again but added little or no substantiating comment to explain why they would have repeated this experience. Nearly 25 per cent of those interviewed qualified their answers in some manner. The most frequent comment was that a year of residence might be highly desirable but that a second year might easily be pointless.

"One year is valuable; two years is too long a time. The counseling service is fine. The fact that there is no sequence in courses is the chief liability."

"The General College is valuable for just one year of background, as a means of getting acquainted with college."

"One year is valuable — not more, however."

For the remaining 30 per cent of the students interviewed, those who felt they would not have voluntarily matriculated, the reason most frequently given was their desire to go elsewhere.

"Perhaps I would have gone to S.L.A. and elected one or two courses here."

"I would have entered S.L.A. and then gone on into medicine. Courses here are too much related, and they don't furnish prerequisites for advanced training."

"S.L.A. would have been more beneficial. Credits from there would be accepted for engineering."

Only a few of the above group gave a categorical no, implying that they considered the program quite valueless for them.

"I would much rather have specific job training."

"I felt cramped in my course selections, for I couldn't take what I really wanted."

"Coming here would be pointless unless direct preparation for nursing could be obtained. It is just a waste of time."

Considering these replies as a whole, about 70 per cent of the students seemed sufficiently convinced of the values of the General College to them to believe they would voluntarily reenter for a year if they had to do it over again. When it is recalled that less than 10 per cent had originally entered of their own choice, it is clear that the program has overcome a strong initial handicap and impressed students with its tangible worth.

In answer to a question concerning whether the year's work had provided some preparation for their present occupational choice, almost half of the interviewed students pointed out some vocational values. As one might have expected from a study of the objectives of the college or the curriculum itself, specific job information and skills were rarely mentioned, students chiefly listing the growth that they had made in personal and social adjustment and the broadened outlook they had gained on many problems. The following comments illustrate this tendency:

"Have become a more interesting person — can talk on many subjects now."

"Rate it very highly. Lawyers need spread in background, as I have observed from my interviews with some lawyers. Journalists too require such broad training."

"General education has given me more poise and self-assurance. I feel a little above high school graduates and as good as any S.L.A. student."

Others voiced uncertainty or qualified sharply the vocational values of such a program.

"Assets — merely broadening. Deficits — not settling down to definite, specific study."

"No, though I got a bit of help from mathematics. A good stiff English course with emphasis on grammar and punctuation would help a good deal. That is the sort of thing I'll need for Technology."

"The values have not been direct and definite for me. I am uncertain as to how much this year may help."

Still other students — constituting a fifth of the group — gave definitely negative answers to this question.

"Courses here have nothing to do with vocational preparation."

"All courses tend to teach you how to spend money, how to spend your leisure — not how to make the money necessary for other activities. Definite prebusiness training would be desirable as a substantial basis for further work."

"No, not at all! More preparation is given here for marriage and home life. No training is given for earning a living."

At the same time that these materials concerning the attitudes of General College students were being gathered, another closely related study was made of the educational adjustments of General College freshmen as compared with those of freshmen in the College of Science, Literature, and the Arts and with those of students enrolled in postgraduate courses at the Miller Vocational High School.[7] The major purpose was to find out whether students who attend schools providing a program of general or liberal education show better or poorer adjustment to their school environment than do students enrolled in a vocational school program. In this study it was assumed that a well-adjusted student is a person who, on the whole, likes his teachers and courses, enjoys his fellow students, participates in extracurricular activities, and feels that the school itself is administered efficiently and fairly. The measure of adjustment used was the Bell School Inventory.

No significant differences appeared among the average adjustment scores of these various groups. Judged by the results of this inventory all three populations appeared to be making a satisfactory educational adjustment to their post-secondary school courses.

Striking differences did occur among these three groups, however, on the extent to which they endorsed certain statements in the Bell School Inventory. As indicated in Table 9, which gives only comparative data on students in the General College and the College of Science, Literature, and the Arts, the dissatisfactions of General College students lie largely in the content of their curriculum, the way in which the subject matter is presented, and the lack of apparent relationship between present courses and their chosen occupations.

In interesting contrast to these relatively unfavorable evaluations of the curriculum were the attitudes expressed concerning faculty-student relationships in the General College. Teachers in this college were much less frequently judged sarcastic than were instructors elsewhere, and General College students likewise did

[7] Bessie S. Smith, "The Effect of Vocational Training on Students' Attitudes toward School," unpublished master's thesis, University of Minnesota, 1940.

TABLE 9. DIFFERENCES BETWEEN GENERAL COLLEGE FRESHMEN AND THOSE ENROLLED IN THE COLLEGE OF SCIENCE, LITERATURE, AND THE ARTS WITH RESPECT TO EDUCATIONAL ADJUSTMENT

Statements from the Bell School Inventory	CR *
Do you like all the subjects you are now taking in school?	2.9
If you were able to do so, would you like to attend some other school than the one you are now attending?	2.9
Do you think your school activities are controlled by too small a group of students?	2.0*
Do most of your teachers make their assignments definite and clear?	2.1
Is this school providing the kind of preparation that you want for your chosen occupation?	5.0
Do some of your teachers "talk over the heads" of their students?	2.0
Are some of your courses very boring to you?	2.8
Are some of your teachers very sarcastic?	2.6*
Do you have difficulty in keeping your mind on what you are studying?	2.7
Have you frequently found the ventilation poor in some of your classrooms?	2.4
Are most of your teachers successful in putting across their subject matter?	2.4
Have some of your teachers criticized you unjustly?	2.6*
Do you think the principal of the school allows the students sufficient opportunity to participate in the administration of the school?	2.1*
Would you like to take a different group of courses than those in which you are enrolled?	2.4

* Unless the critical ratio is marked with an asterisk, General College students gave the larger percentage of replies indicating dissatisfaction.

not feel that they had been subjected to much unjust criticism. They also believed they had been given a real share in the administration of the college. In fact, the report of this study concludes, "the attitude of these students toward the curriculum is quite dissatisfied; toward the staff it is very favorable." [8]

The study made by the University Committee on Educational Research of the attitudes of freshmen and sophomore students throughout the state toward their college courses provided a final comparison of the attitudes of General College students and those enrolled in the College of Science, Literature, and the Arts, the division which most General College students had hoped to attend. As Table 10 shows, the two groups of freshmen rated almost identically the value of their first college year. Approximately the same percentages of both groups were enthusiastic about what college had meant to them; very similar percentages confessed disappointment with what they had found. When

[8] *Ibid.*, p. 46.

TABLE 10. EVALUATION OF COLLEGE EXPERIENCES BY STUDENTS ENROLLED IN THE COLLEGE OF SCIENCE, LITERATURE, AND THE ARTS AND IN THE GENERAL COLLEGE

Ratings	First Year of College (Percentages)		First Two Years of College (Percentages)	
	S.L.A.	G.C.	S.L.A.	G.C.
Very disappointed	5	5	2	2
Slightly disappointed	22	22	16	12
What I expected	25	21	21	14
Favorably impressed	30	33	37	33
Highly favorable	17	18	23	39
No response	2	2	1	..

comparisons were made of the attitudes expressed by sophomores in the two colleges, it was found that General College sophomores gave somewhat more favorable evaluations than did the arts college sophomores. Although too much weight ought not to be attached to these subjective and perhaps hasty judgments, it is highly impressive to find that General College students, most of whom do not enter the college voluntarily, close their work with attitudes fully as favorable as those expressed by arts college students.

ATTITUDES OF FORMER STUDENTS TOWARD THE PROGRAM

When former students were asked whether or not they had gained greater understanding or skill in each of the four basic areas of out-of-school living as a result of their General College residence, they attached most value to the help they had obtained on socio-civic problems and on those relating to personal adjustment, as may be seen in Figure 28. The fact that the contribution of the college in the area of vocational adjustment was judged to be far less valuable corroborates the opinions of present students and is understandable, since the college program emphasized vocational orientation and not job preparation. Chapters 7 to 10 give specific observations and criticisms made by former students in support of the generalized ratings of help given in these four areas of life activity. When asked in another question whether they felt that they were better off in some way because

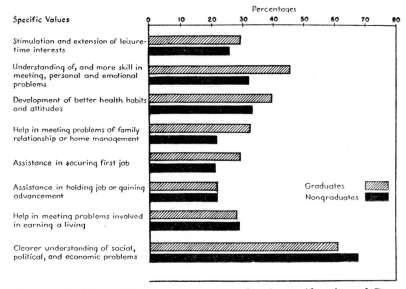

Figure 28. Opinions of former students concerning the specific values of General College courses.

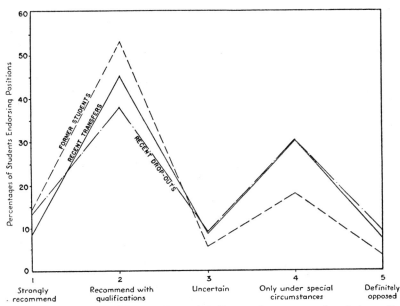

Figure 29. Responses of former General College students concerning their readiness to recommend the college to prospective students.

187

of their General College experience, three fourths of these former students gave an affirmative answer.

Finally, all the former students — those who had recently left college to look for work, those who had been out several years, and those who had transferred to other colleges — were asked the same question that had been used in interviews with present General College students: Would they recommend the program to other young people of similar interests and abilities? The distribution of responses, given in Figure 29, was distinctly bimodal. Former students listed more assets than liabilities in the program, but they definitely felt that recommendations should be qualified. The qualifications that they listed agreed closely with those pointed out by the students now in school (in particular that the program is better suited to women students, to the student who can spend but one year at the university, and to the student whose vocational goal demands primarily a sound general education).

The hundreds of free-response comments made in support of these recommendations were carefully analyzed by three judges and then classified under certain major rubrics. As may be seen in Table 11, the strengths of the program that were most frequently noted by these former students were that General College courses provided important orientation to college work, to advanced courses, and to future employment; that this type of general education was valuable for practically all students; that the General College offered certain courses that were excellent in content, interesting, and well taught; and that the program was especially valuable for those who have not made a definite vocational choice. The weaknesses or liabilities most often noted by those who had attended the college were these: that the program did not lead to or prepare for specialization and hence could not be advocated for those who have well-defined interests and abilities; that the required work was often of a low standard of quality, which almost any student can meet with a minimum of effort; and that the college did not provide specific vocational courses that would aid in securing employment.

TABLE 11. STRENGTHS AND WEAKNESSES OF THE GENERAL COLLEGE PROGRAM AS INDICATED BY COMMENTS OF FORMER STUDENTS *

Strengths	N	Per Cent	Weaknesses	N	Per Cent
Provides a general program which is valuable to practically all types of students........	77	18.5	Does not lead to specialization, so it cannot be defended for those who have definite abilities	74	17.8
Provides a program which is valuable to those who have not made a definite vocational goal	46	11.0	Lacks specific vocational courses which help in securing employment	44	10.6
Offers certain courses which are excellent in content, interesting, and well taught.......	45	10.8	Requires work of a low standard which almost any student can do with a minimum of effort	43	10.3
Offers certain courses which are an excellent preparation for life activities..............	41	9.8	Wastes the time and money of the students who attend and gives no useful training........	40	9.6
Offers courses which provide orientation to college work, advanced courses, and future employment	40	9.6	It is difficult to get credit for work done in General College, so it is best to transfer as soon as possible	38	9.1
Provides a valuable program for those not entering professional or specialized fields.....	34	8.2	Offers courses too general, too elementary, and not very helpful......	36	8.6
Offers courses which help an individual to discover his own abilities and interests........	30	7.2	Draws students who are indifferent, have no purpose, have low ability, and give the college poor atmosphere	36	8.6
Provides a general program especially valuable for girls	19	4.6	Has a poor reputation which is detrimental to the students in the college......	30	7.2
Provides a program valuable for those who can spend only one or two years at the university	14	3.4	Forces students with low qualifications to take program even though they may want to enter some other college......	21	5.0
Offers work which helps an individual to make social adjustments and to work effectively with others	12	2.9	Offers some courses which are both uninteresting and useless as well as poorly taught......	20	4.8

* Four hundred and sixteen former students not only made a general rating of the values of the program but also added some type of free comment, explaining their attitudes. Thus 18.5 per cent of all these students stated in varying phraseology their belief that the General College provides a program of general education which is valuable to practically all types of students.

OUTCOMES OF GENERAL EDUCATION

SUMMARY

The attitudes that young people express toward their college experiences need to be interpreted in the light of many other evidences, since the actual impact of a curriculum on students may be far different from the influences the students attribute to it. Nevertheless it seems reasonable to believe that students who are in the midst of an educational experience are in a peculiarly advantageous position to identify its strengths and weaknesses.

Taken as a whole, the present findings are probably quite similar to what might be found in any college. Some young people are keenly enthusiastic; many others are moderately favorable; still others are relatively indifferent or inarticulate; a few are openly antagonistic. The largest assets of the General College program, in the eyes of its students, are the thorough concern for youth that pervades both teaching and counseling activities, the interesting and practical character of many of the courses, and the readiness of teachers and administrators to work with the students, sharing with them the actual development of the program. The liabilities seem to be inherent in the oversimplication of subject matter, the extensive overlapping among various courses, and the assumed lack of articulation of the courses with their future jobs or with advanced college work.

Although General College students find many things wrong with their courses and a number of them frankly state that they would not recommend the program to a friend or a younger brother or sister, they are no more iconoclastic in these evaluations of their college than are the young people enrolled in liberal arts colleges throughout Minnesota or in the College of Science, Literature, and the Arts at the University. As many evidences presented in this study indicate, General College students actually appear a little more ready than other students to attribute positive strengths to their college experiences. When it is remembered that the majority of young people come to the General College under some measure of compulsion, the favorable appraisal given by most students indicates that this program of general education has made notable strides in selling itself to its consumers.

CHAPTER 12

Summary and Implications

The General College at the University of Minnesota differs in many ways from the typical institution of higher learning in America today. In the first place, it was established to provide an appropriate type of education for groups of young people comparatively new to our American colleges — young people whose needs do not seem to be met by either the traditional liberal arts curriculum or the various professional schools. By establishing a separate college for students of moderate academic talent or uncertain vocational orientation or those with a real desire for general education, the administration hoped that more attention could be given to their individual and special needs. In this way it might be possible to identify those young people who should rightly be encouraged to continue their work at the university as well as those young people who should be aided in making a more immediate adjustment to out-of-school opportunities and responsibilities.

Perhaps the most significant aspect of the General College experiment, however, has not been the conscious attempt to meet the learning problems of these new groups of students but rather the development by this faculty of a new program, a so-called *general education curriculum*, designed to prepare young people for the unspecialized phases of living, outside and beyond the classroom. Although these courses were evolved primarily for students of limited scholastic potentialities, most of them appear equally promising for abler students. Some of these new courses have a specific or single subject-matter core — such as biology, physics, chemistry, psychology, art, sociology, political science, and history — but they were planned to be much more than popularizations of the traditional liberal arts content. Instead they represent fundamental reorganizations of the subject matter involved, with emphasis on contemporary events and everyday applications. For example, General College instructors have sought to increase the students' knowledge of the principles of physical science that apply to their own environment, to extend their knowledge of health, to make them more aware of current political, economic, and social issues, to render more effective their control of such basic skills of communication as speech and writing, and to develop their understanding and appreciation of contemporary and familiar art. Other General College courses provide instruction in areas almost totally neglected by the liberal arts college. Thus the new orientation courses, drawing their content from a wide variety of the traditional subject-matter fields, have been consciously designed to help students to develop a better understanding of the problems of personal and social adjustment, family living, the choice of and preparation for a career, and civic and community service.

The General College has also differed impressively from the majority of our American colleges in the emphasis that has been placed on personnel work. It was the first college on the university campus, for example, to extend the usual aptitude testing program to include measures of achievement in several fields — measures of vocational interests, of personality traits, and of social attitudes. Likewise it has studied intensively the activities, interests, and needs of its present students and of young college-trained adults, thereby discovering facts about the backgrounds and abilities of young people that are not usually available to college instructors. From the very beginning of the General College program the faculty have generously given much of their time to individual conferences with students, discussing not only educational and vocational problems but personal matters as well. Since 1935 a central counseling office, composed of two full-time counselors and several graduate assistants, has supplemented and vastly extended the efforts made by the faculty to counsel and advise their students.

For all these reasons — the types of young people served by the college, the new general education curriculum evolved for them, and the strong emphasis placed on individual guidance and counseling — an inquiry concerning the successes and failures of this experimental program is peculiarly significant. Inasmuch as the General College has become a prototype for many general education programs elsewhere, the discovery of its essential strengths and weaknesses should assist markedly in developing appropriate curriculums for the ever-increasing numbers of high school graduates who seek at least a year or two of college training.

A two-year appraisal study was therefore begun in September 1938, the same year that the four new orientation areas were introduced into the General College curriculum. The very fact that the curriculum itself was in a state of flux necessarily complicated the task of evaluation. Other difficulties lay in the inadequacy of the instruments available for measuring certain desired outcomes and the limitations of time and resources necessary for studying comprehensively this program of general education. At the very start it was decided rather to investigate as many outcomes as possible than to examine a few of them exhaustively. As a result, the present study has been essentially exploratory, providing a general picture of the values of this particular curriculum to the students themselves.

DEVELOPMENT OF OBJECTIVES

A first essential task in making this appraisal was to identify and render as explicit as possible the goals of the General College program, so that evaluation might be focused on objectives judged important by those actually responsible for the curriculum. The tentative formulation of goals set forth in Chapter 3 was developed by a committee, working with statements of objectives provided by the entire staff. As a survey of these goals indicates, the staff is genuinely concerned that students achieve a larger measure of self-understanding, happier and more wholesome family and social relationships, and an intelligent perspective on social and economic issues. Faculty members also frequently mention the student's attainment of a valid vocational choice and a deepened appreciation of the world of work. Definite vocational preparation or training is seldom specified as a goal, since the charter given the college was for the development of general rather than vocational education, nor do these statements of objectives emphasize the definitely intellectual values that are assumed to accrue from systematic study in subject-matter fields. On the whole, the detailed objectives outlined by the present staff appear very similar to those principles and goals that have guided the development of the program from its beginning.

THE STUDENTS AND THEIR PROGRAMS

Another major task was to study the kinds of young people served by the college so that any gains they made in knowledge, skill, or appreciation might be interpreted in the light of their characteristics at entrance and the type of educational experiences that the college provided for them. Evidences from many sources helped to define the backgrounds, abilities, and interests of these students and their success in this general education program.

General College students come predominantly from upper middle-class homes in the Twin City area — homes in which the cultural level appears to be somewhat, but not markedly, above that of the typical American home. With respect to the quality of his secondary school work and his performance on tests of aptitude or academic achievement, the average General College student is surpassed by approximately two thirds of all Minnesota high school graduates. On the American Council Psychological Examination, for example, he ranks at approximately the tenth percentile of the students enrolled in the College of Science, Literature, and the Arts and at the thirty-fifth percentile of all junior college populations. Hence it is not surprising to find that most students who come directly from high school are referred to the General College because of low grades or low test performance; the one student in five who has had college work elsewhere, amounting in most cases to less than a year's study, usually comes because he has been dropped or placed on probation in the college of his initial enrollment.

In contrast to their academic handicaps, General College students show a somewhat better general social adjustment than young people at large, resembling closely, in these personality traits, other University of Minnesota students. In social attitudes they are also similar to other college students. Likewise, in recreational interests General College students appear rather typical of young people included in youth surveys elsewhere. At entrance to college, for example, they read magazines such as the *Saturday Evening Post, Time, Life, Reader's Digest, Collier's,* and the *Ladies' Home Journal.* On the radio they listen predominantly to variety and popular music programs. A good many students take part in organized sports. Most of them belong to two or three clubs, chiefly of a social type, with a sizable minority holding some position of leadership in these organizations. But few of them have developed hobbies of any sort.

Almost half of all General College students have hoped initially to be admitted to the College of Science, Literature, and the Arts; about a third designate other colleges as their first choice; a seventh state that they have planned from the beginning to enter the General College.

The overambitious educational plans outlined by these young people at entrance to college are equaled only by the lack of realism in their vocational choices. Almost half expect to hold professional or managerial positions. Despite the obviously inappropriate nature of these goals, most students state that their choices are fixed or reasonably fixed. In addition, two thirds believe that the university, and the university alone, will prepare them for their life work — an expectation certainly not peculiar to the General College population.

The typical student actually remains in the General College for only one year. This short length of stay results in a large turnover in the student population and complicates enormously the planning of instruction. During their General College residence students vary greatly in the extent to which they elect courses in the major areas with which this particular general education program has been concerned. For example, 15 per cent of the students have had contact with only one, two, or three of the eleven comprehensive areas, whereas another 15 per cent have taken at least one course in eight, nine, ten, or eleven areas. The

courses most frequently elected are those in the areas of individual and vocational orientation, psychology, current affairs,
and literature, speech, and writing, whereas less than a third take
courses in the areas of physical science, general arts, home life
orientation, or euthenics. Frank reports from students suggest
that they are not overburdened with academic work. The absence of clearly defined and consciously adopted goals in many
courses sometimes leads to rather casual work habits, for not a
few students do most of their studying before the midquarter
and final examinations.

About a third of all the General College students who remain
in college for one year do not take any comprehensive examinations, despite the fact that the passing of three comprehensive
examinations each year is required for normal progress toward
either a degree or transfer. During the eight-year period studied,
however, there has been an encouraging increase (from 25 to 40
per cent) in the numbers of students who take three examinations
at the end of their first full year's work. Approximately one student in five meets the requirements for the Associate in Arts
degree, although less than 15 per cent actually apply for and receive it. One student in four elects more than six quarters' work
at the university, either in the General College or some other
division.

CHANGES IN STUDENTS' INFORMATION, ATTITUDES, AND ADJUSTMENTS

A third important undertaking, which presented far greater
difficulties, was to explore the specific character of the changes
in students' information, attitudes, and off-campus activities that
occur during their attendance at the General College. Since most
students elect courses in two or three of the orientation areas and
since these areas now appear to be the core of the entire curriculum, outcomes of instruction in these fields were studied
with special care. Tests were selected or constructed to assess
certain characteristics and were administered at the beginning
and at the end of one year to both freshmen and sophomores.
It was thus possible to discover how much a year's instruction
at either level contributed to students' growth. Gains over a

two-year period could be studied only for a few characteristics tested at the very beginning of the evaluation. Changes in scores were then studied by covariance techniques, permitting isolation of the contributions made by particular educational experiences. Since students who dropped out of college during the year were not retested, the outcomes described below apply only to those who spent at least one year in the General College.

In such basic skills as English usage and reading, the typical student at the end of the sophomore year betters the record he made at entrance to college. However, when the gains made by General College students on the Cooperative English Test are compared with the gains made by students in the College of Education or the College of Science, Literature, and the Arts, adjustments being first made for differences in ability, the non-General College students show some superiority. This is undoubtedly due to the very different objectives and processes prevailing in other colleges, English being required of all students and much greater emphasis being placed on grammar and usage.

During a year of residence in the General College students gain in their understanding of the problems dealt with in the four orientation areas — those involved in personal adjustment, home and family relations, vocational orientation, and socio-civic affairs. For example, the typical freshman, whether or not he is enrolled in the special courses designed to promote these outcomes, advances to approximately a seventy-fifth percentile score in the entering freshman distribution. These end-of-the-year scores are strikingly similar to those made by entering freshmen of much higher academic competency enrolled in the College of Science, Literature, and the Arts. The fact that students who elect the orientation courses gain significantly more than those who do not take these courses indicates that special instruction effects a deepened understanding of these problems. Furthermore, sophomore students who took any of the orientation courses the preceding year show excellent retention of the knowledge they gained, thus giving some evidence of the validity and reality of the materials used.

Information and understanding that students possess concerning contemporary affairs are also definitely increased by residence in the college. In this respect General College young people appear distinctly superior to other campus groups, after necessary statistical adjustments are made for differences in academic ability. Those enrolled in the special socio-civic orientation courses make higher scores in these tests than those who are not, the advantage being decisive on the sections most closely related to the orientation courses.

The social attitudes of students, on the other hand, seem to be far less affected by residence in the General College. Because this lack of change is also characteristic of students in the arts college and the College of Education, it is possible that these changes take place more slowly or that beliefs and opinions are much less amenable to direct influences than are the specifics of information. The measured personality traits of General College students likewise show little alteration during the year. Analysis of scores from the Minnesota Personality Scale reveals no change on the family and the health and emotionality sections, a significant loss on the morale section (which perhaps should be interpreted as a gain, since many students needed to readjust their overambitious goals and plans), and a significant gain on the social adjustment section. This latter gain is corroborated by results from the Bell Adjustment Inventory, in which students gained significantly in two areas (social adjustment and emotional adjustment) of the four measured. It has not been possible, however, to trace these gains to specific courses or combinations of courses.

A year's stay in the college does not measurably affect recreational interests. Thus the activities in which these young people participate frequently at the beginning of the year still remain the things they characteristically do at its close. Whatever gains have been discovered are largely in the field of sports and physical exercise and in social activities of an informal sort. Nor is there much evidence of alteration or improvement in their free-time reading or radio interests, although this may again be a slow-change factor. Perhaps one of the most disturbing findings is the little use General College students make of the rich extra-curricular resources for general education that are available on the university campus. Unfortunately no comparative data exist for other colleges, to indicate whether liberal arts and professional school students were any more alert to these opportunities — if indeed they were as much so.

As the year progresses, students' educational plans tend to become considerably more realistic. By the end of the year, for example, fewer students expect to enter the College of Science, Literature, and the Arts, and many more look upon their General College training as a terminal education. Vocational plans are not correspondingly altered, however, at least to the extent that might have been expected. Although there is some scaling down of the overambitious plans outlined at entrance to college, the careers that many young people decide upon are still quite out of line with their measured abilities. Moreover, most students remain unduly optimistic concerning the salaries they hope to earn in the years ahead. A vocational orientation course is of some assistance in eliminating job choices in the upper professional categories but it does not appear to help most students to make new choices suited to their interests and abilities. On the other hand, when instruction of this type is reinforced by individual counseling, students emerge at the end of the year with definitely more appropriate vocational choices.

STUDENTS' ATTITUDES TOWARD THE GENERAL COLLEGE

A fourth task has been to determine the attitudes of students toward the General College as an institution. Although such opinions yield only a subjective appraisal of the program, they at least suggest its impact on the students most intimately acquainted with it.

In appraising the program as a whole, students show by their comments distinctly favorable attitudes. More than two thirds of the group would enter the college voluntarily if they were again confronted with the choice — even if they were free to go elsewhere. A minority would recommend the program without qualification to a younger brother or sister; many others acknowledge important positive values of the program. The most valuable outcomes, according to students, are found in the areas of general orientation and of social understanding and adjustment. The most frequent criticism is lack of attention to problems of job readiness. Ratings made by students in the General College and in the College of Science, Literature, and the Arts concerning the value of the time spent in college reveal that the two groups cannot be differentiated in their appraisals of their freshman experiences but that General College students give somewhat more favorable estimates of the value of their second year of study. The fact that General College students complete their work with attitudes that are as favorable as those held by liberal arts college students becomes more striking when it is recalled that most of these young people do not enter the college voluntarily.

When students are asked to name the courses that have helped them most, the majority mention broad survey courses of a subject-matter type and courses in speech. These are commended for their clear organization, interesting content, and the challenge they provide for further study. The courses held in least repute are most often scored for the rudimentary nature of the material, the evident overlapping with other courses, and the poor discipline in the class.

All the evidence indicates that faculty-student relationships are exceptionally happy in the General College. Part of this excellent rapport must undoubtedly be attributed to the amount of time faculty members spend in counseling. Thus students report an average of four conferences a year with their faculty advisers — far more counseling and personal advisement than is listed by students in the College of Science, Literature, and the Arts or in most other liberal arts colleges in Minnesota. Again and again students have commented very favorably on the personal concern shown by faculty members about their vocational choices, plans for continued study, or avocational activities. In addition, more than 60 per cent of all General College students also have one, and usually several, conferences with members of the central counseling office. Those who have received this aid are almost unanimous in their high commendation of it and their appreciation of the counseling service.

SUMMARY AND IMPLICATIONS

The ultimate measure of the worth of the General College program must be found in what students think and do after they leave college. In the present appraisal only a first exploration of these residual outcomes of education could be made. Fragmentary but highly suggestive evidences have been gathered concerning the interests, attitudes, and activities of almost 700 former students. More than 250 of this group had been out of college from three to seven years and were either homemakers or workers or unemployed. Their responses to items included in a sixteen-page questionnaire, modeled after that used by Pace, suggest how the out-of-school interests, activities, and needs of former General College students compare with those of young people of similar ability who had followed the usual liberal arts curriculum for one or two years and who had been out of college about the same length of time. The other 475 former students had left the General College more recently, a minority (160) to take work in other divisions of the university, the rest to seek jobs. These recent withdrawals supplied less detailed information, relating chiefly to their further educational and vocational experiences and to their appraisal of the General College program. Since they had been out of college only a short time, no comparisons were made with Pace's results. In the brief summary that follows, the leading findings for these various groups are presented in the same order as that used in Chapters 6 through 10 — their readiness for continued learning, their orientation to personal problems, their home and family living, their vocational readiness, and their socio-civic competence.

Students who continue their education on a full-time basis after leaving the General College are in the minority, though many others take some additional courses, mainly of a vocational type. Thus less than a fourth of all General College students transfer to some other unit of the university, and these are quite definitely, and appropriately, superior in terms of scholastic ability. They remain in the colleges to which they transfer for an average of four quarters, with the result that half of all transfer students have either obtained degrees in these new units or are still working for them. Among those who have dropped out of college recently, one in fifteen is attending some type of school. Those who have been out of college from three to seven years, including both the graduates of the General College and students who left without completing the program, have done considerably better. Out of every ten such students, four report some further technical or business training, two have had some other college experiences, and one has taken some correspondence or extension courses, usually vocational in nature.

Although no personality tests have been readministered to students out of school several years, to find out how competent they are to cope with personal and emotional problems, almost half of all former students say that their General College experiences have assisted them in meeting such difficulties successfully. Many even describe specifically the kinds of help they have received.

The reading and recreational activities in which former students engage have also been explored and compared not only with those of students now in school but, whenever possible, with those of young people who attended other colleges for one or two years. The findings reveal that young people out of the General College several years read the same magazines, by and large, as do entering freshmen. Young people now in school more frequently read such magazines as *Time, Newsweek, Life,* and the *Woman's Home Companion,* and the former students broaden their interests to include *Better Homes and Gardens, American, Good Housekeeping,* and *McCall's;* but these are the only significant differences. Those who have completed the General College program do not read books and magazines that are any different from those read by students who drop out. Reading habits are apparently not markedly affected by an additional year's contact with the program.

The radio-listening tastes of former General College students appear somewhat more elevated than those of students now in school, whose interests center largely around variety and popular music programs. Those out of school for some years, for example, listen frequently to such programs as *Information Please,* the *Ford Sunday Evening Hour,* and the news comments of H. V. Kaltenborn. Yet when the radio interests of former General College students are compared with those of young people of similar ability who have dropped out of the colleges with more traditional programs, it appears that, although differences are slight, the former General College students have probably somewhat less educated radio tastes.

About three fourths of all former students are members of clubs or associations. Church and betterment groups head the list; civic and political clubs are very infrequently mentioned. Study groups of any sort are notably absent.

In the area of home and family living it is rather surprising to find that young people out of the General College several years show the same kinds of interests and the same degree of participation in activities as do those who dropped out of other divisions of the university in earlier years. On the other hand, former General College students seem to be more intelligent in their health practices than young people trained in the traditional programs. For example, more General College young people have hospitalization insurance, take regular exercise, and plan for medical and dental care. In addition, more than a third of these former students cite ways in which General College courses have helped them to develop better health habits and attitudes.

When they leave school, few General College students obtain jobs requiring specialized skills or knowledge. Sales work predominates, followed by jobs in the clerical field or in semiskilled trades. In contrast to the 50 per cent of entering freshmen who select vocational goals classified in the top two categories of the Minnesota Occupational Scale, approximately 6 per cent of the recent drop-outs and only 12 per cent of those out of school from three to seven years hold such jobs or appear to be advancing toward them. In their occupational activities and interests students who receive the Associate in Arts degree can seldom be distinguished from those who leave the General College before graduation. In measured job satisfaction the two groups are also markedly similar. When the job activities and attitudes of General College graduates of earlier years are compared with those of young people who have dropped out of other colleges, only a few differences appear, such as the greater frequency of sales jobs among former General College students and that of supervisory and clerical jobs among students in the other group. The latter students appear to be definitely more satisfied with their work. In neither group is there much appreciation of the need for knowing more about social trends and changes that may affect their jobs.

In the field of opinions and attitudes toward economic, political, and social problems, the fact that former General College students hold views closely allied to those expressed by entering students suggests that instruction on fundamental social outlooks has had a small immediate effect. Yet two out of every three former students are quite thoroughly convinced of the value of their General College experiences in clarifying the meaning of social, political, and economic problems. The same patterning of socio-civic activities is found when former General College students are compared with those still in school or with those who have dropped out of other colleges of the university. The interests of all groups are directed mostly toward large national issues rather than toward specific local problems, and participation in socio-civic activities is usually limited to routine duties.

Students who have been out of college from one to seven years express much the same attitudes toward the college as do those still in school. When asked whether or not they would now recommend the college to a younger person, a good majority are on the favorable side. The most frequent qualifications are that the program is better suited to the student who can spend but one year at the university, to the woman student, and to the student whose vocational goal demands only general preparation. More than four fifths of all these former students feel that they are better off in some definite way because of the time they spent in the General College.

This, then, is a summary picture of all the evidence obtained concerning the General College program. Taken as a whole, it is a reasonably favorable one. Despite the fact that the average student remains in the college for only a year, he comes to like it and to attribute real values to its curriculum and its counseling service, many of which are attested by searching measures of his knowledge, skill, and interests, and by the actual activities in which he engages. That so many positive outcomes are apparent after a single year's residence seems highly significant. Such results should be definitely encouraging to colleges that have an opportunity to work with their students two, three, or even four years and that are willing to develop personnel and planned curricular systems.

Certainly whatever discouraging or disquieting findings have emerged — and there have been numerous such discoveries, particularly with respect to the postcollege activities and interests of students — are by no means peculiar to this program. Any college staff that honestly attempts to study the degree to which its goals have been realized in young people's patterns of thinking or living is bound to find similar wide discrepancies between goals and actual attainments. In contacts limited to a year or two years, it is probably impossible for even the best educational program to compensate for many of the deficiencies brought about by long years of inappropriate home training and by an overly bookish high school education, unrelated to the demands of out-of-school living. When gaps appear, therefore, in the pattern of outcomes for which the General College faculty has labored so hard, they can only serve as a challenge to more imaginative and persistent efforts to attain the desired ends.

In conclusion, it must also be remembered that the present evaluation has been limited to the students directly served by the General College. No attempt has been made to determine the tremendous impact of the General College on the rest of the university. The addition of new courses in other colleges dealing with contemporary problems — in art, for example; the expansion of projects begun in the General College, such as the newsreel theater, music listening hours, art exhibits, to all-university functions; the impetus given to university-wide personnel services — these are only a few of the ways in which the General College has enriched and enlivened the life of the whole university. Nor has any accounting yet been made of the wide influence of this program in setting the theory, pattern, and practice of general education throughout the country.

IMPLICATIONS FOR GENERAL EDUCATION

The implications of the present findings for the further development of the General College program — and for other general education programs elsewhere — are many. Undoubtedly one of the most difficult tasks that faces higher education in the United States today is the development of a type of educational program from which students of moderate academic talent can profit. Faced with this problem the General College at Minnesota developed new types of courses in the social studies, especially in the area of current social and economic problems; courses in the application of sciences to everyday life; courses in the arts of communication; and courses in the understanding and appreciation of contemporary art, music, and literature. Later it developed four basic orientation courses dealing with personal problems, vocational adjustment, home and family problems, and socio-civic affairs. Broad-gauged examinations to measure understanding in these areas have indicated that students with moderate academic talent can and do profit significantly from this type of educational content. Moreover, sophomores who took the courses the previous year made almost as high scores as freshmen just completing their instruction, suggesting a high retention of these insights. Students' own opinions testified to the value of the courses, and former students praised especially the emphasis on contemporary problems.

The present findings thus clearly demonstrate the value of instruction that has been clearly focused on goals important to the student. Since growth can be stimulated by experiences specifically organized toward a given end, as was shown so impressively in the field of current affairs, each college faculty and student body faces the challenging task of determining the particular kinds of outcomes they will strive to achieve. Developing such a truly functional curriculum must always be a long, arduous task, for subject matter must be selected and new learning procedures formulated in terms of their significance to the individual. In such pioneering the General College has accomplished a great deal, but to gain a fuller understanding of the problems involved, many more colleges will have to experiment with the innumerable possible methods for suiting educational experiences to the backgrounds and abilities of average young people — the kinds of young people who will make up the vast majority of the workers, the homemakers, and the citizens of tomorrow.

Another major problem of general education centers in the need, common to so many students, for fundamental educational and vocational reorientation. Students expect traditional courses, expect to receive bachelor's degrees, and believe that college will fit them for entrance into the top-ranking occupations, a conviction usually shared by their parents. These problems of reorientation were especially acute in the General College, since 80 or 90 per cent of the students had initially enrolled under some form of compulsion. To meet this situation the General College developed an extensive personnel and counseling service, a system of faculty advisers, and special offerings in vocational orientation. An evalution of these services has indicated that students' educational objectives do become scaled down to more realistic levels and that the combination of individual counseling and a special course in vocational orientation results in a marked tendency toward realistic choices of future occupations. Students in college as well as former students give enthusiastic tribute to the helpfulness of faculty advisers and the special counseling services of the college. Moreover, in spite of the fact that only a small fraction of the students enter the General College voluntarily, the typical student, after a year's residence, is as convinced of the value of his experience as is the typical student in the College of Science, Literature, and the Arts; those who have spent two years in the General College are even more convinced of its value.

A third major concern of general education is found in the problem of students' personal and social adjustment and in their social attitudes. The present appraisal reveals that students with limited academic talent obtain as favorable a rating on measures of personal and social adjustment as do students endowed with a much greater degree of academic ability. During residence in the General College, moreover, they gain in these traits in about the same degree as their academically superior colleagues. Almost half of the group of former General College students also indicate that their self-understanding and personal and social adjustment have been aided in many important ways by their General College experiences. An examination of individual case records in the counseling offices would unquestionably provide further evidence of helpful assistance with respect to personality and adjustment. The fact that the gains manifested with respect to attitudes and personality traits are much smaller than those shown on informational measures may be explained in several ways — the unreliability of the tests used, the deep-seated, emotionally toned nature of many of these beliefs and attitudes, developed through long years of home and earlier school experiences, and the absence of as much positive emphasis throughout the entire program on these more intangible outcomes of education. A more forthright attack by the college on the development of mature, reasoned attitudes toward personal and social problems might do much to improve this situation. Until students have been further stimulated through special counseling and through the whole instructional program of the college to develop a working philosophy of life, no marked change can probably be looked for in these areas. From General College experiences, what seems most effective in gaining this end is not any particular course or combination of courses but expert personal counseling added to a college atmosphere in which sympathy and a concern for the problems of the individual are constantly apparent.

A final major problem of general education is to provide a learning environment from which there will be a maximum transfer of the insight and understanding gained in class to activities and interests that characterize life beyond the classroom. The problems of appraisal are especially difficult in this area, for one cannot assume that the school is directly responsible for adult activities, interests, and attitudes. Such things are more properly attributed to the total pattern of society and culture than to one aspect of it. But a college is indeed an ivory tower of isolation if it is not actively concerned with the extent to which understanding and insight are manifested in the adult behavior of its former students. There were, perhaps, discouragingly few evidences of such manifestations revealed by this evaluation study. Although there was, for example, evidence of improved health practices and better social adjustment, there was no particular evidence of improved civic and political activity or of improved leisure-time interests, such as reading and radio listening. This general lack of difference between former General College students and those who left other divisions of the university after two years is not surprising, even though it is highly disquieting, when one reflects on the years that all these students have spent in cloistered school environments, the little direct attention given these problems by even the most alert teachers, and the innumerable forces at work through families, friends, and such agencies as the press, the radio, and motion pictures to stereotype the pattern of out-of-school thinking and living. True, the General College has not yet succeeded in developing all its desired outcomes, but this failure is fully shared by the traditional arts colleges. Pace discovered that the only area of out-of-school living differentiating the interests and activities of students who received bachelor's degrees from those who dropped out of school was the vocational one. The largest differences among college graduates and nongraduates concerned the amount of money earned.

Probably it is only as college experiences are conceived as life itself, rather than as preparation for life, and only as students come to believe more thoroughly that college experiences are meaningful to them beyond the classroom, that the gap between school and community can be effectively closed. The experience in general education at the University of Minnesota does not provide a definitive suggestion for achieving this goal. It is possible that college programs of general education need to be accompanied by specific job training, actual work experiences, and more frequent and varied contacts with the community and the world beyond the campus.

Many kinds of experiments must thus be undertaken before colleges discover how to make available the most effective education for their young people and to assist them in formulating realistic educational and vocational choices, in developing wholesome personal and social attitudes, and in transferring their classroom learning to the thousands of specific situations that will confront them outside the college. The present study reveals impressively the need for continuous appraisal of all the means used to achieve these ends in terms of what they contribute to the thinking and living of students. As ways are increasingly provided for teachers to observe what happens to young people, immediately and in the first difficult years of adjusting to the responsibilities that await them beyond the classroom, and for students to participate actively in gathering and interpreting such evidence, a new vitality should come to classroom teaching and learning. Educational programs will then be continuously shaped to stimulate and guide the growth of young people in the ways best suited to their individual and special needs and to the demands of full and happy living in a democratic society.